TIPS & TRICKS
FOR DOG
OWNERS

BY HERTA PUTTNER, D.V.M. AND EVA ROHRER
TRANSLATED BY WILLIAM CHARLTON

CONTENTS

ACQUISITION

Do not let yourself be "seduced" by an awkward puppy with adorable eyes before you have carefully considered that you are also taking on the responsibility for a living creature, which needs enough space, attention, food, and care. The dog will suffer badly if you were to neglect or even push it away, if you got tired of it. Ask yourself if you are prepared to organize your life around the dog, to make it possible for it to live in an appropriate fashion, and if necessary to give up something for the sake of the dog.

Do not let yourself be "seduced"

Before you acquire a dog, all family members should approve. Otherwise there will be tension and arguments, which in the end the dog will have to pay for, if someone rejects it or it is given away to an uncertain future.

The family must approve

Ask your landlord if you are even allowed to keep an animal in your apartment. Check your lease to see if you have signed an agreement not to keep animals in the apartment. In private homes and homes with yards, in principle you are allowed to keep animals as long as they do not disturb the neighbors.

Are you allowed to keep an animal?

When your circum-stances change

If you are facing a substantial change in your life circumstances, whether you are expecting a child or are planning to move, you should not acquire an animal. You may have too little time and so much to do that the dog will come off the loser. This is particularly true in the beginning when the dog needs your attention to adjust. If it does not get your attention, it often reacts by exhibiting behavioral problems, becoming unhousebroken, or chewing on the furniture and carpet.

Which dog for which pocket-book?

When choosing the right dog, you should also consider how much you can and want to spend on the new family member. If you have limited financial resources, it is better to buy a small dog to keep the food costs low. If you want to hold down costs, choose a dog that does not have to go regularly to the groomer — after all, costs for clipping and plucking increase three to four times a year! Also, do not forget the cost of vaccinations and visits to the veterinarian!

Which dog for which person?

Dogs are gregarious animals — just like humans — which is why the four-legged friend has a particularly easy time in becoming attached to the family. For the dog, the pack is the family who accepts it. Obeying an instinctive hierarchy, it accepts one family member as the leader. It usually behaves in different ways toward the other members of its "pack."

Puppy or older dog?

• Puppies are more suitable for younger people and families with children. Older people are easily overtaxed by an all-too lively young dog, which "gets into every-thing" and needs plenty of exercise. Fully grown calm animals, on the other hand, may feel uncomfortable with noisy children and commotion in the daily routine.

- Dogs make extremely valuable companions for children: they teach important lessons and become an addition to childhood. Children who grow up with dogs behave more socially than those who do not. They learn to be considerate to a weaker creature and to accept responsibility. They also have a playmate they can cuddle with when they are sad. Parents must be prepared to recognize the dog as a family member and to support the child in the care of their four-legged friend.

Dogs for children

consideration ✳
Responsibility ✳

Breeds that make suitable companions for children include the Beagle, Airedale Terrier, Labrador Retriever, Collie, Puli, and other retrievers.

- An older, quiet animal is the ideal companion for senior citizens. Older, infirm people may likely be overtaxed by larger, powerful animals. It is better to buy a small dog. Animal shelters are crowded with abandoned older dogs, who are waiting for a good home and a kind mistress or master. Breeds that make suitable companions include the Pekingese, King Charles Spaniel, Maltese, Yorkshire Terrier, Lhasa Apso, Tibetan Terrier, Dachshund, and all smaller half-breeds.

Dogs for older people

Do you hate to exercise? Anyone who hates to exercise should not buy, of all things, a Greyhound or some other large, temperamental four-legged friend, who must get its exercise on long walks!

Does barking bother you? Even small dogs can cause problems when they bark. Anyone who likes his peace should choose a quiet, older dog with a deep voice, so as not to be disturbed by its barking.

Strength and the ability to assert yourself You should acquire a large, powerful dog only if you have the corresponding strength and ability to assert yourself. You can get into serious trouble if your four-legged friend will not walk on the leash and you cannot keep it under control. With or without the leash, the dog may happen to injure somebody.

Female or male? Unwanted offspring are easily prevented today. Therefore, you should decide based on the character traits of the animal, which sex you prefer. If you want a four-legged friend that is more independent and not as affectionate, then you should choose a male dog. Male dogs are also more likely to fight with rivals, which is why they need someone who can handle them consistently. If you would rather have an affectionate, devoted animal, you will get more pleasure from a female, who will also be easier to train. A female does not have to go outside as much (to "relieve itself"), in contrast to a male who must go out not only more frequently but for longer periods of time as well. It is in his nature to mark his territory and to sniff around much more.

Female Dogs Are:
- *More Effectionate*
- *more Devoted*
- *Easier to Train*

MALEs Are Dogs Arc:
- *more Aggressive*
- *less Effectionate*
- *less Independent*
- *need more time out*

8

You should walk a dog for a half hour at least twice a day. Your four-legged friend will do more, however, than simply relieve itself. It also needs plenty of exercise to stay healthy, and it also revels in the many smells. Dogs are pronounced scenting animals. For dogs, smells provide a wealth of important information, which they use to find their way around.

Outdoors twice a day

A long walk is good not just for your fellow-lodger but for you as well. So, you should also look forward to this time, or at least force yourself to go even when you sometimes do not feel like going. This regular exercise is also essential for your health, as any doctor will confirm!

A dog needs contact with its owner and sufficient exercise. Although a yard is ideal, particularly for large four-legged friends, it is no substitute for attention. If you leave a dog alone too much, it will feel lonely and spiritually neglected. You must walk your companion twice a day, devote time to it, and care for it.

Do you have enough time?

If you are very punctilious, you should carefully consider the acquisition of a dog — particularly a long-haired dog. Any dog naturally tracks some dirt into the house, and you may have to vacuum up hair several times a day. This, of course, takes more time, which is no obstacle for a true animal lover.

Hair on the carpet

Large, powerful dogs do not belong in small apartments! The larger the city and the residential block, the smaller the dog should be. In any case, even more important than the size of the apartment is the opportunity for exercise!

If you live on an upper floor and do not have an elevator, you should not choose a breed that is prone to disorders of the backbone, such as the Dachshund or Basset Hound.

Large dog: yard

If you love decidedly large dogs, such as the Great Dane, Giant Schnauzer, or Saint Bernard, it is best to have your own yard. These dogs, however, are also good watchdogs. (Do not overlook, however, the expensive food costs.)

Where should you buy?

Watch out for unscrupulus sellers. Buy a dog from a source where you get a health guarantee.

Animal shelter or breeder

If you take a four-legged friend from the animal shelter, it will thank you with much love. Sometimes these dogs are somewhat difficult or timid at first, because they usually have had bad experiences with people. Therefore, do not give up right away. Have patience! These animals, when they finally have good experiences, become particularly affectionate and devoted.

You can also buy a pedigreed dog from a reputable breeder. You can obtain addresses from, for example, your local kennel club. Ask your neighborhood dog owners for their advice.

A reputable breeder will love his dogs and will not treat them simply as merchandise. He will never have too many animals, because otherwise he could not provide them all with proper care. The breeder will take good care of his dogs. He will be interested in making sure that the puppies find a good home with their new owners, and will give the future "master" or "mistress" tips and advice on nutrition. The breeder will have no objections if you stop in a few times to check on the puppies' progress. The breeder will not try to talk you into taking a particular animal. He will not take the puppies away from their mother before they are 8 to 12 weeks old.

Puppies from the breeder

Never buy a dog through the mail! These dogs are bred on a large scale in a sterile, inappropriate environment. They scarcely have any contact with humans. To make these operations as profitable as possible, the puppies are often sent away after only 6 weeks. Because of this the puppy does not go through the essential socialization phase with its litter mates. The puppies often suffer not only physical harm (cooped up in a cage with too little water and too little food), but psychological damage as well. Furthermore, you will end up with a dog that you have never personally seen.

Stay away from mail order dogs!

You have arranged a time to pick up the dog. Now is the last moment to set up everything for the new arrival. Buy a light collar, a leash, water and food dishes, and an ample supply of suitable food.

You have made your decision

A quiet place to sleep The dog needs a quiet place to sleep that is free of drafts and where it can go whenever it wants. A mattress on a slatted frame makes a suitable bed for larger dogs, and a medium-sized or smaller four-legged friend needs a sleeping basket of adequate size (consider how large the puppy will be when it is fully grown!). Keep in mind that puppies chew on sleeping baskets, because this is how they get rid of their baby teeth.

Not on stone floors Do not let the dog sleep on stone floors! The rising cold can all too easily cause your four-legged friend to develop a kidney infection, which can be very painful.

The dog in the yard If you want to keep a watchdog in the yard, you must provide it with a sufficiently large, weather-tight dog house. The entrance of which faces opposite of the weather side. The floor and walls should be well insulated (double walls filled with, for example, fiberglass insulation).

You can also put a mattress inside the dog house or cover the floor with straw.

Keep in mind, however, that the dog can protect you best when it is inside the house! Barking from inside the house is more likely to scare off a burglar, because he will not know exactly where the dog is. Above all, at night and particularly at low temperatures in the winter, you should at least leave your four-legged friend in the foyer of your home, and give it a place to sleep there.

Most accidents happen within your own four walls. When your four-legged friend arrives in your home, you must arrange your household in a suitable manner.

Puppies, in particular, are very inquisitive and get into everything — just like children. Put anything that could be dangerous to the dog out of reach.

- Always store detergents and cleansers safely.
- Never leave pointed or sharp objects lying around.
- The same applies to the garden (shards of glass, gardening tools, fertilizer, and herbicides).
- Puppies also enthusiastically chew on telephone and electrical cords. Put cords where the puppy cannot "attack" them.
- Secure stairs.
- Secure swimming pools and garden ponds.
- Inspect fences.

Bringing home the dog you have chosen is an exciting moment. It is exciting for the dog as well, whether it is still a puppy or already fully grown. You should have enough time to prepare for the event. It is beneficial if you can take a few days' vacation to make the adjustment easier for the new arrival.

Examine your future companion closely one more time for possible health problems. Have the breeder or owner give you

Is the puppy healthy? the vaccination certificates, so that you know which diseases the animal is protected from, and when the next vaccinations are due.

Traveling by car Bring along a family member or a person you trust, who will sit in the back seat on the trip home to keep your four-legged friend company and comfort it if necessary. This reduces the dog's fear and makes it less likely to vomit.

Drive carefully! Drive slowly and carefully, and occasionally stop for a while if it is a long drive. This way your new companion will get used to driving, and later it will willingly get back in the car.

The puppy explores the home After the puppy has arrived in your home, give it time — it must first sniff out its new home properly — to get used to its new environment. Do not smoke, and avoid noise and commotion! Even if your children are overjoyed to have a new playmate, explain to them that they must behave quietly, or the dog will become nervous and frightened.

The dog is very thirsty In your general enthusiasm do not forget to give your four-legged friend water right away. Put a water dish in the spot where it will always find its water.

Play only when it wants to You should only play with the dog when you can tell that it wants to, when it, so to speak, "asks" you. Remember that puppies also need a great deal of sleep.

Do not scold the dog — particularly a puppy — if it has an "accident." As a precautionary measure, lay down plastic where your four-legged friend stays. Dogs are clean by nature!

An "accident" can happen to anyone ...

Puppies often howl the first night in their new home because they miss their mother and the warmth of their siblings. A little trick to comfort the puppy in the beginning: Put the basket or mattress near your bed the first night and put a thickly wrapped hot-water bottle in the puppy's bed.

It is lonely without mother

You will frequently pick up and carry the puppy (or small breeds). When you do so you should always observe the following: one hand supports the hindquarters, and with the second hand you hold the dog at chest height (with the thumb between the front legs).

Carry puppies the right way

Never lift or pull the dog by the front legs. Dogs do not have a collar bone. The shoulder and trunk are connected only by muscles and tendons, which can be strained by picking the dog up incorrectly (also by too much jumping).

You must never exclude your four-legged friend from the family unit! You are now its family. So, it would be animal cruelty to exile the puppy in an empty room. In this way it could become disturbed and neurotic.

You are now its family

Even a well-trained dog must, of course, be kept on a leash in the city. The noise of traffic, people streaming by, a dog in heat,

Out and about with your

15

four-legged friend

or playing children could easily distract or frighten it. It could injure someone or run in front of a car and cause an accident. Remember that you would be held liable for the damages.

The dog's side: the edge of the sidewalk

Always walk your dog on the edge of the sidewalk nearest to the gutter. In this way it will not disturb other pedestrians and will not relieve itself in the middle of the sidewalk, which will also help to spare the anger of the passers-by.

Play it safe

Allow your dog to run free only where you can be sure that nothing can happen to it, and that it will not threaten other people. Muzzle the dog if cyclists and joggers are in the area.

A trip to the country is a special treat, and the open countryside entices the dog to romp around. Nevertheless, keep the dog on a leash when you are in or near a forest. A warden could consider your four-legged friend, even if it is harmless and friendly, to be a danger to the game animals and shoot it! Some wardens are particularly ruthless and will exercise their right to shoot dogs, suspecting that the dog is being used to run deer.

To keep the dog from becoming a problem

It is certainly unpleasant to step in dog excrement. Other far more serious problems can result, however, when this causes people to object to dogs. Be as it may, the dog is not to blame for the problem, the owner is. Therefore, some fellow human beings unjustly rail at dogs. So, it is up to you not to make the situation worse through improper behavior.

If it is not possible for your four-legged friend to relieve itself on undeveloped land, where it will not disturb anyone, train it as early as possible to use the gutter exclusively for this purpose—but you still must scoop.

In some cities there are already vending machines with sacks and scoops to clean up your dog's "business." You can also bring along a bag and a piece of cardboard to clean up any messes the dog makes on the walk.

Sack and poop– scoop

Stay away from children's playgrounds! In no case may your four-legged friend do its "business" in the sandbox. This would be like putting gasoline on the fire for dog haters. Their protests and complaints would truly be understandable. The problem would again be blamed on the dog, which is only following its instincts to bury its feces in the sand.

Play– grounds are off limits!

ANIMAL SHELTERS

Animal shelters are over-crowded
Often it is mixed-breed dogs that wait for a new owner in animal shelters. The four-legged friends in the usually overcrowded shelters have very little space and need attention from people. It is essential to find them a kind master or mistress quickly. Representatives of many animal shelters make an effort to do this on televised, local community service programs.

It is in your hands
Animals are abandoned or given away because they do not fit in the vacation plans, their owners have grown tired of them, they have been trained incorrectly, their owners cannot cope with their bad habits, and so forth. For these reasons, we warned so emphatically about misconceptions and asked you to consider carefully whether you really will and can do everything that is required for the dog. Do not forget that the owner is always to blame when animals exhibit behavioral problems or cannot be controlled.

Every dog has a story
Many dogs have already led a life of suffering, have had bad experiences, or suddenly lost their beloved master or mistress because of illness. Accordingly, the dog can be good-natured, fond of children,

hostile to children, trusting, timid, or anxious. Some are used to having a yard, others only an apartment. Some are fond of cats, while others become aggressive at the sight of them. Examine the animal closely, and discuss with the staff of the shelter which dog is suitable for you.

Anyone who is very fond of dogs gives them time to adjust and creates a pleasant atmosphere. By showing patience and giving the dog attention, you will soon have made friends even with difficult dogs. At first do not let your four-legged friend run free or allow others to pet it. Do not expect it to put up with changes to its familiar surroundings before you become better acquainted with it, and know how it will react in particular situations, what it likes, and when caution is called for.

Get acquainted

At the animal shelter you will fill out a questionnaire and answer questions about many requirements and conditions. You will be asked about your family situation, the conditions in your home, and how much time you have available for a dog. Do not view this as harassment. These questions are essential to make sure that the dog finds the right home and does not soon end up back in the shelter. You too will learn something about the animal and will be able to form a better impression.

Applicants who are notorious for treating animals badly or have absolutely no good qualifications should not get a dog. Anyone who, for example, would like a difficult dog without having experience with dogs should choose a better-suited four-legged friend.

May you return a dog? If the dog turns out to be impossible to train or discipline, you may have to give it up. Accordingly, you should not rashly subject the four-legged friend to further disappointment. When it cannot be avoided, however, you must return the dog to the place where you got it. If you know of a better place, inform the first place about what you are doing.

When problems arise When you have a problem, all animal shelters, as well as local community service television shows, will gladly help you with tips and advice. Some dogs are returned only because the new owner did not consider a few fundamental things, and the four-legged friend snapped at him. You should follow these tips by Edith Klinger when you take possession of an animal whose prior history you do not know or do not know well:

- Initially, always keep the collar on the dog. With particularly difficult animals also keep a short leash on top. This way you can grab it at any time, without having to hold the dog, which may not tolerate this at first.
- Do not pet it at first. It may stay still for a short time, but will then snap at you in fear, because it has had bad experiences with the human hand. Do not pet the dog until you are certain that it knows that nothing will happen to it.
- Do not reach for the dog while it is eating.

It could think that you want to take its food away again.

- Never take food away.
- While playing fetch, always use two sticks. In this way you can always throw one without having to take the other from the dog's mouth. Otherwise, it may snap at you.
- When someone rings the doorbell or knocks at the door, it has the urge to guard. Do not hold it back by the collar! Lock it in another room.
- If the dog growls (or snaps) occasionally, take note of the situations and avoid them. Never stand in front of the dog while staring at it and scolding it. This will only make it feel more threatened! The best method: turn around. For example, say, "Come, let's go for a walk!" in a calm, firm tone of voice and walk away. Do not remain standing.
- Do not force it away from its "territory" (sofa, armchair, and so forth). Instead, lure it away with a treat.
- Do not offer food to it under the table without speaking to it first. Otherwise, it will not know to whom the hand belongs.
- Do not "wrestle" with it!
- Never touch an older dog, which may no longer hear as well as it used to, before you have spoken to it. Approach only from the front.
- Do not take anything away. The dog considers it to be prey, which it will defend. Coax it away only!

THE CHILD AND THE DOG

Less anxiety, more responsibility
Dogs assume an important position in the lives of children. They are more than just playmates. Children develop a close relationship with their dogs. They learn to take on responsibility and to show consideration for other's needs.

Comfort and attention
Children can find comfort in their four-legged friend when they are misunderstood by adults. They find it easier to deal with tension and anxiety. To a certain degree the dog can even replace the absence of siblings. The dog's great advantage: it is always there and always has time.

For difficult, disturbed children who do not make friends easily, the relationship with a dog is a form of therapy!

Guardian and "personal trainer"
The dog in turn protects the child and exhibits faithfulness and devotion. The dog demands exercise, and sees to it that the children, who are far too inactive today, do something for their health. The dog and children alike, however, should follow certain rules in their life together.

Play with me!
Dogs are great models in play. Time and again they inspire children to come up with

new ideas, whether running in the yard or wrestling in the house.

Starting at what age?

Children can already be captivated by a dog at about one year of age. Up to kindergarten age, however, you should not let your children play alone with the dog. It can happen that the dog frightens the child, or the child could grab the dog clumsily or frighten it with screeching, possibly causing the dog to nip.

How old should the dog be?

Basically, you can also take adult dogs, such as those from the animal shelter, without any problems if they are fond of children and the children are no longer very small. These are often very unfortunate four-legged friends, who become especially devoted when you give them a good home.

The advantage of puppies is that they are there from the start and, so to speak, grow into the family. Then the relationship between the four-legged friend and the child becomes particularly close. Nevertheless, you must start training the puppy very early.

The dog is not a disposable toy

You must explain to older children that the dog is not a toy that they can simply discard when they please, but a playmate who they must take outside in any weather, and who regularly needs food and care.

Although the dog loves company and also romps around enthusiastically with the children, it also needs a quiet place where it can withdraw and be "safe" at times from noisy, boisterous children.

Can children care for the dog by them- selves? Before the children start school, they, of course, are not ready to take care of the dog or to take on responsibility (at this age the children do not yet have authority over the dog). They should, however, help you with the feeding and care of their four-legged friend, so that this becomes a natural job for the children.

Give them an early start ... Once the children are about eight years old, you should start to hand over certain chores to them. You should supervise them while, for example, brushing the coat or setting out the food. Most twelve-year-olds can take care of their playmate alone.

Dogs hardly obey children Dogs hardly obey children because they do not have any authority yet. Once the children are about seven years old, they pass the dog in the pecking order, but the dog will still not obey them properly.

Walk the dog alone? At about 14 years of age, most children can already walk the dog alone. The dog should be trained and accustomed to obeying commands from the young "mis- tress" or "master." Otherwise, there could be problems during encounters with other dogs.

A baby is on the way If you are expecting a baby, you must give the dog exactly as much attention as be- fore, and not suddenly neglect it. Other- wise, it could react with jealousy to the addition to the family. Nevertheless, you must make it clear to the dog that it is lower in rank than the new arrival. You and your four-legged friend must both see the baby as the focus of the family. Then its protective instinct will come to the forefront, instead of its jealousy.

Some animal owners also have a bad conscience, because the baby is the focal point, and become particularly attentive to their four-legged friend while the baby sleeps. However, this can lead to misunderstandings. To the dog this means: when the baby is awake, my owners ignore me; only when it is away (sleeping), do my owners pay attention to me. This could lead to real jealousy toward the new family member. It is best to feed and pet the dog in the baby's presence. This way it will associate a pleasant experience with the child.

Keep your "paws off" the baby!

You must also put clear restrictions on the dog regarding the baby. The crib, toys, and pieces of clothing must be off limits for the dog. Never let the dog, no matter how small and lovable it is, sleep with the baby. Avoid this not only for reasons of hygiene, but because your four-legged friend could possibly try to defend "its" place against the baby.

Healthy dog, no danger

Observe hygiene. Objects that the child touches often should be cleaned frequently. Vacuum the floor or carpet frequently, as soon as the child can crawl around the house. This does not mean, however, that you should get into a panic about hygiene: A healthy dog is no danger for humans!

Inappropriate behavior is to blame, not the dog

Some people with children are negatively disposed to dogs. They have heard or read that children have been jumped on and been badly injured by dogs. Such accidents happen, however, because of the inappropriate behavior of the children. In general, dogs are fond of children, as long as they have not already had bad experiences or have been deliberately trained to be "vicious."

Dogs are not toys

Most accidents happen when children play with a dog, or want to pet it. They unintentionally hurt it or grab the dog in a way that it finds unpleasant. Then the dog often reacts with a warning bite. With children up to five years of age, the head and neck are in danger, mostly because of their small body size.

More responsibility on both sides

According to accident statistics, if dog owners would show more responsibility and parents would explain to their children important rules for handling dogs, many accidents could be avoided.

Dangerous peculiarities

Dog owners are responsible for their animals. Only they know the peculiarities of their dogs, and understand what they do not like, what makes them aggressive, and so forth. Accordingly, they must supervise their dogs.

In approximately 70 percent of incidents between dogs and children, the owner is not in the immediate vicinity. The leash or muzzle laws in public places are obeyed too little.

Activities such as running, playing on a swing, roller-skating, and cycling often trigger the hunting instinct of the dog. In such situations the dog owner must put his animal on the leash, if he knows that the dog is "susceptible" to this.

Children as "prey"

Many bites are by "repeat offenders." This is due mainly to the rearing and training of the dog, and which tendencies are strengthened or weakened. You must not permit snapping in puppies. This seems harmless with a cute puppy, but it is already practicing for later . . .

Snapping is not allowed!

- Keep the dog in accordance to its species, breed, and age. Give it the necessary attention and an appropriate space to exercise in.
- Secure and handle the dog so that other people are not threatened. Keep nervous dogs and those that may be inclined to bite on a leash and muzzled.
- Never leave the dog alone with strangers, especially not with children.

Three requests of the owner

There are certain important points that every parent must teach his or her children about dealing with dogs. This is particularly important when the child's own dog lets them do virtually anything. Children then believe that all dogs are as good-natured. Do not make the child afraid of dogs, but explain to the child what our

Parents must pay attention to this

four-legged friends like and what they must watch out for.

What dogs dislike

- Dogs can be nice playmates, but are not toys. They could attack and bite you, were you to yank on the tail, the ears, or the collar or stroke the coat against the grain.
- Pet strange dogs or those who do not know you well only when the owner is present (only he or she knows whether the animal might attack), and the dog is wagging its tail in a friendly way as it approaches.
- Do not approach from behind. The dog likes to know with whom it is dealing. Also, let the dog sniff your hand.
- If you are romping around, running, playing on a swing, or riding a bicycle and a dog approaches you, it is best to come to a stop or to move very slowly. If you do not move wildly, and simply ignore the dog, you become unattractive to the dog as "prey," and it will leave you alone.
- Never disturb a dog while it is eating, or take away its toy, because it will react aggressively. This is in the dog's nature.
- Never enter a yard that is guarded by a dog before you have contacted the owner.
- Should someone happen to be attacked—even if it is only a scratch — for safety's sake you should go to the doctor. That is, if you cannot locate the owner and do not know if the dog has been vaccinated against rabies.

UNDERSTANDING

Do not make the mistake of viewing the dog as a "four-legged" human. Then the dog will feel misunderstood, and you may possibly think that you have a "bad," poorly trained dog on your hands. You must understand the dog, and then deal with it. Then it too will understand, and you will have a lot of fun with each other.

Not a "four-legged" human being

The dog is anything but poor in its means of expression. Because of its good hearing and unbelievable sense of smell, it lives in a different sensory world, which could not even be expressed in words. It does this through its posture, visual cues, sounds, raising its hair, and so forth. These behavior patterns are instinctive and are broadened by the association with its siblings, and later in its new family. In jest we often say that the dog and its master are alike.

The dog lives in another world

Never stare at the dog (and especially not with your eyes wide open), particularly in moments of real danger. In dog language, this means that you are ready to attack. Do not try this to instill respect in the dog. This may work with humans, but the dog does not recognize this meaning.

Do not stare

Barking my be bred in

When a dog barks, this does not necessarily mean that it will attack. Certain dogs, such as the Dachshund and terriers, were originally bred to bark frequently. Barking can also be simply the expression of joy, such as when you are preparing to take a walk . . .

"Stay away from me!"

Before you approach a dog, you must be certain of its mood. The posture of the ears and tail says a great deal: beware if the dog lays its ears back, draws in its tail, and bares its teeth, even if only a little. You must not cross over the "critical distance." Friendly words will not do any good either. Dogs that behave in this way are so-called fear biters, and are desperately reckless if you get too close.

Raised arms mean I am ready to attack!

Extreme caution is called for when dealing with guard dogs. The dog is trained to attack aggressively. The signal to attack is, so to speak, the raised arms. This, however, is precisely what people automatically do (especially children!): We hold our arms in front of our face to protect ourselves.

Friendly jumps or attack?

Usually a dog is not attacking you when it jumps at you, assuming that you have not made it angry. Jumping up is usually a sign of joy, a greeting, or the desire to play. The dog, of course, cannot know that you do not want its paw prints on your new clothes.

TRAINING

Responsible dog owners should teach their dog a few important fundamental concepts and rules of behavior, which will make their life together easier. After all, you will certainly want to be able to take your dog everywhere, without these excursions ending in catastrophe. At least not arousing the annoyance of your fellow human beings. With a well-trained four-legged friend, you can even take the wind from the sails of stubborn dog haters.

Good behavior — the best weapon against dog haters

Prerequisite for successful training: Not drilling or harshness (which could make the dog neurotic), but patience and consistency produce the best results. It is in the dog's nature to please its "leader" (pack leader), so it is not all that difficult to teach some manners if you have the necessary ability to empathize.

The dog wants to please

When you acquire a puppy, you must begin with training very early on. Once a dog develops bad habits, it is not easy to break it. Therefore, do not let the lovable puppy do something that you do not want it to do as an adult dog.

Training the puppy

Act like the mother dog

When you want to forbid the puppy from doing something, it is best to act like the mother dog. Pick it up by the scruff of the neck, give it a few shakes, and then remove it from the place in question.

Beating instills fear

Do not yell at the dog: it will not understand. Correct it with "Bad" or "No" in a loud, firm tone of voice. Also, you must never beat the dog. It will not make it obey, but rather make it timid and shy. Beating causes some dogs to bite out of fear. One other thing: from the owner's hand should come only food, medicine, and kindness!

Correct immedi– ately

Important! Basically, your correction must follow its bad behavior immediately. Otherwise the dog will be confused, because it does not know why you are correcting it.

Praise lavishly

The first commandment in the training of your four-legged friend: Praise it lavishly when it has done something well; have patience if it takes somewhat longer for it to learn something, or occasionally forgets something. Practice until the dog remembers it.

Short and sweet

Use short sentences and as few words as possible. It can memorize them and associate them with a particular situation or behavioral pattern. It does not understand longer "explanations."

Who is the pack leader?

The dog by nature needs to take a definite place in a community. The master or mistress assumes the role of the "pack leader." These people should always take the lead, or the dog will be tempted to play the role of "leader."

Particularly in the beginning, only the mistress or the master should be responsible for training. This will help the dog learn faster. Different trainers could confuse it, if they do not act in exactly the same way. Children are less suitable, because they have too little authority.

Only one trainer

What the dog learns during play, it will find easier to remember. Furthermore, the dog will not tire as quickly when it learns during play. Whenever possible, you should incorporate training with play. Then the dog will also remain eager to learn, long after it is fully grown.

Learn during play

Do not practice any exercise longer than about five or six minutes, to avoid overtaxing the animal. Always use the same commands! After it eats it must rest a while, and you must wait until later to start practice.

Do not overtax

The first thing every puppy should learn, of course, is its name. This is the best way to teach it: Put it on a long leash. Each time you call it, gently pull it toward you. When it reaches you, you must praise it lavishly. A small treat — appropriate for dogs — encourages success.

This is how it learns its name

You can and should train even very young puppies. In certain obedience schools for puppies they are already taught commands. Most importantly, however, this gives the

Kinder-garten for puppies

puppies the opportunity to become acquainted with other dogs. It is important for the puppy to have contact not only with people but with others of its kind as well. This makes even timid, shy dogs more self-confident and teaches them to interact with others of their kind.

The owner also learns in obedience school

At about one year of age, dogs are ready for the so-called "primary school." Not only the dog will learn there, the owner will as well. The owner learns to better understand his or her animal, and to train it more easily with little tricks. Furthermore, the owner can ask the experienced teacher about minor individual problems with the dog.

In training, the dog's inborn talent is promoted, and by working together the master or mistress and four-legged friend will forge a close bond.

An accident, what should you do?

An accident can happen out of fear, or joy, or because the little fellow recognizes and marks the house as its territory. Furthermore, puppies cannot control their bowel movements until they are about three months old. Show the dog its deed immediately and correct with a strict, loud "Bad." But never dunk its nose in the puddle! It will not understand this, because it has done nothing wrong with its nose.

You must get rid of the smell

For whatever reason a particular place was soiled, you should always clean the spot with a disinfectant, so that the odor of the mess does not encourage new "deeds."

Decide ahead of time on a spot in the yard where your dog should relieve itself. Do not correct if accidents happen a few times.

This is how to house-break the dog

At first, take the puppy outside about every two hours. In any case, always take it outside after meals. Praise it lavishly as soon as it relieves itself. In this way it will soon understand what you expect of it.

If you watch your puppy closely, you will notice when it has to "go." It will start to sniff around, circle, and then sit down. Carry it outside immediately at the first sign.

Watch closely

If you live in a high-rise building and cannot get outside fast enough with the little fellow, set up a place inside with newspaper where it can do its business.

Toilet on the balcony

Housebreaking goes hand in hand with getting the puppy used to the collar and leash. The dog must be on the leash when you go outside with it, to keep it from running into the street unexpectedly, or something else from happening. Basically, you may only allow the dog to walk without the leash when it obeys the most important commands.

Get the puppy used to the leash right away!

At first the dog will view the collar and leash as foreign bodies, which it will want to get rid of, because they limit its freedom of movement. In the beginning, put the collar on for a short time and associate it with a pleasant activity, such as eating and playing. Only when the dog no longer tries to get rid of the collar, should you put it on a leash. It is best to do this in the house or yard.

Do not tug on the leash, but rather let your four-legged friend lead you (by way of exception!). However, to stress it one more time: Puppies may do this only until they get accustomed to the leash. Unfortunately, you also see many older dogs dragging their "master" or "mistress" behind them, which is not fun for either. This is a habit that you absolutely must break the dog of!

The "business" must not disturb anyone

Make sure that from the start the dog does its business only in appropriate places. So, pick out a suitable place ahead of time. A suitable place would be the gutter or possibly near bushes and trees, where there is no danger that a passer-by could step in the pile. Otherwise, you will only promote negative feelings toward dogs, who of course can do nothing about it. So, it is up to you to prevent this.

Why does a fully grown dog become unhouse-broken again?

Even if a dog is already fully grown and has been housebroken for a long time, it can happen that it will suddenly have an accident inside the house. Do not react with scolding and anger. A fully grown dog does not become unhousebroken without reason. Consider what problems could have caused your four-legged friend to do so.

An infection of the bladder or the urethra could be to blame. If this is not the case, there are many other reasons why the dog could become unhousebroken:

The dog can become unhousebroken if you leave it alone for an unusually long time or if the time for its walk is long overdue. It can no longer hold its bladder.

Insecurity: If, for example, you move or a new dog moves into the neighborhood, your dog could become unhousebroken. In this situation it will want to proclaim its territory by "marking" it. With some patience this will soon pass. Go frequently to the chosen proper place, and praise your four-legged friend as soon as it relieves itself.

When too many other dogs do their business on the route you take to walk your dog, a timid dog may prefer to use the house as a toilet. Then it is best to take another route that is not as heavily frequented.

Fear and pain

If your four-legged friend becomes frightened while urinating or defecating, or if its leg hurts when it tries to lift it, it could associate the shock or pain with relieving itself. It could become so afraid that it will only relieve itself when it has no other choice (and this can be precisely in the home).

Take it outside frequently. Important: Speak to it reassuringly and praise it when it has done its business. In this way it will soon realize relieving itself will have no unpleasant consequences.

Lazy dog owner

If the "master" and "mistress" are too lazy to walk the dog, and only bring the dog just outside the door for it to relieve itself, they are training the animal to be unhousebroken. After all, the four-legged friend would prefer to stay outside longer. To allow this to happen the dog will hold in its urine and stool. The master and mistress will then think that the dog does not have do go. So, they bring it back inside, where the accident then happens.

Prevention: Do not return to the house as soon as the dog relieves itself. Keep the dog from thinking that the length of the walk depends on when it relieves itself.

Frequent reason: jealousy

Was your dog sick? If it was, it probably received more love and attention than usual. It now wants to bring back this attention with little surprises in the form of accidents. Four-legged friends often behave in the same way when another pet or a baby arrives, with which they now have to share the owner. In this case it is best to ignore the dog and to act as if you have not even noticed its deed. Clean the spot only when it is not around. Prevention: Do not neglect your four-legged friend!

"Accidents"

When dog owners always yell at their four-legged friends, the dog occasionally becomes so submissive that it becomes unhousebroken out of utter confusion. This goes back to an instinctive behavior in the pack.

Such a poor animal absolutely belongs with a lovable new "master" or "mistress," if the owner is not prepared to change his or her behavior.

Dogs are pack animals and get lonely if they are alone too much or receive too little attention within the family unit. Under this neglect they suffer so much that they would rather be scolded than receive no attention at all from their owner. Accordingly, unhousebrokenness is its last resort to get attention. It should not ever come to this. Set aside an hour a day for your four-legged friend, or at least ask another family member to spend time with the animal.

Is the dog alone a great deal?

Some dogs are so much the center of their owner's attention that they protest being ignored immediately with an accident. Furthermore, they are not afraid to "demonstrate" on clothing, shoes, or handbags, and in unfamiliar homes as well. The excitement that the dog triggers in this way increases its importance.

"Center of attention" dog?

Remedy: Correct the dog immediately, but if possible do not create a sensation.

Some dogs do not have particularly strong nerves. Excitement, as well as great joy, can cause it to lose control of its bladder and sphincter. You can help your dog to gain self-confidence by praising it lavishly — for example, when it performs well during training sessions.

When the nerves fail

A dog must obey certain commands so that you can maintain control in dangerous situations, making social interactions easier. "Sit," "Come," "Heel," "Bad," "Out," and "Stay" are the most important commands. Praise, correction, and commands must differ clearly in tone. Express commands firmly and clearly.

Starting at what age can you teach commands?

Approximately at an age of 10 to 12 weeks you can begin to practice with "Bad!" and "Out!" Later, practice "Come!" and "Sit!" (first at home). Practice each command a quarter of an hour a day for about a week, and in the meantime repeat regularly what has previously been learned. After every correct reaction, praise the four-legged friend!

Little tricks in training

Training requires patience and concentration, but also a few psychological tricks to make teaching and learning easier.

Use chance

When you watch your dog, frequently it will do things by chance that you will want to teach it. If you then immediately give the appropriate command ("Sit," "Down," "Come," and so forth) and then immediately praise it lavishly, it will very quickly associate the command with its behavior and will learn more easily.

Use body language

When giving each command, also use a particular posture and hand signal. This will strengthen the command, and your four-legged friend will then also know how to react, for example, to a particular hand signal. Furthermore, it will not obey someone who shouts "Here!" and fails to give the appropriate signal.

If you see that you are making no progress during a practice session, you must encourage your dog from time to time. It is best to do an exercise that it can do well and likes to do. If you then praise it lavishly, you will also be successful with other exercises.

Prevent learning frustration

Do not give up if an exercise is unsuccessful. The dog will immediately take advantage of your "weakness," and will repeatedly try to have its own way. If it is absolutely necessary, you can substitute with a different exercise. For example: If the dog does not want to go into the house, carry it in. If the dog does not "heel," it must do so on the leash, and so forth.

Do not give in

Never scold the dog if it has not done anything wrong. It will not understand it. It associates correction only with the activity that it is currently engaged in. Correct the dog only when the dog is not supposed to do something!

Praise and correction

The same is true of praise. Praise your four-legged friend only when it is doing something that you have commanded it to do. It will not understand if you praise it simply because it is not behaving badly. This will only confuse the dog. In other words, praise only for acts, not for omission.

Praise only for a reason

Two essential commands that even the very young dog should learn are "Bad!" and "No!" It is very important, however, that the dog does not confuse these two commands.

Always forbidden

There are things that are absolutely forbidden, that is, things that the dog may never do (for example, correct with "Bad!" if it relieves itself in the house, jumps on strangers, and so forth).

Forbidden right now
Some forbidden acts should only apply in certain situations, for example, going into a friend's kitchen. If you correct with "Bad!," the dog will not know what to do, because in your home it is allowed to go in the kitchen.

Command not carried out
If you also use "Bad!" when you want to teach the dog to sit, for example, but it goes to you anyway, the confusion is complete. "Bad!" then means to the dog that it may never do it. If the dog cannot relate "Bad!" unambiguously, soon it will no longer obey you at all.

It is of decisive importance, however, that you use one word for acts that are absolutely forbidden, another for acts that are forbidden at the moment, and a third for the incorrect execution of commands.

It must learn to drop objects
When a dog gets something in its mouth, it will rarely give it up. If the object is food, it will not give it up at all. This is instinctive behavior. Nevertheless, your dog should learn as soon as possible to give up what it has in its mouth. This is particularly true if it growls as it defends the object. First, by doing this the dog is trying to displace you from your higher position in the pecking order (if it succeeds in doing so, it will do what it

wants). Second, the dog could manage to get hold of poison bait, sharp bones, or some other dangerous object that you will have to take away from it.

This is how to teach your four-legged friend to drop an object: Say "Out!" loudly and clearly. Then hold the muzzle from above and press the flews against the teeth. If it releases the object, praise it lavishly. If it growls, shake it by the scruff of the neck. Do not conclude the exercise before it releases the object. Otherwise, it will be the winner.

Practice until it releases the object

Watch to see when your fellow-lodger sits on its own. Then immediately give the command "Sit!" so that it associates the command with the act of sitting.

This is how it learns "Sit!"

Naturally, you cannot wait each time for the dog to sit on its own. In this way, however, you will reinforce the active training: On your command "Sit!" press the hindquarters of your four-legged friend gently, but firmly downward.

Practice first inside the house. Move a short distance away from your dog and give the command "Come!" clearly. If the dog comes to you, praise it immediately. Practice the exercise several times in succession, then take a break. If the dog does not obey the command, you must "persuade" the little fellow with a trick. Take an appropriate treat (not candy) or the food dish, walk away, and repeat the command "Come!"

This is how it learns "Come!"

Mistakes with the command "Come!"

There are puppies that while taking a walk on the leash suddenly come to a stop or lie down and refuse to continue on. If you now stop and start a "discussion" with your four-legged friend, it will think that it has you under control. Subsequently, it will stop more and more frequently.

Never pick up the little rebel and carry it for a stretch! Otherwise it will no longer walk outside at all. Continue on your way. You will pull it along a short distance, and it will realize that it cannot achieve anything when it stops. As soon as it walks, praise it lavishly. The message to the dog is: If I go on, I get attention, and if I remain sitting, I get nothing.

Some owners give the command "Come!" as an invitation to come along, but remain standing themselves and wait to see if the dog comes. The dog cannot understand this. On the command "Come!" you must immediately move in the desired direction.

This is how it learns "Here!"

With the command "Here!" you customarily call your dog back from a greater distance. For this exercise you need a long leash (approximately 15 meters long). Leave your four-legged friend sitting, and go as far away as possible. Then give the command "Here!" loudly, and tug lightly on the leash until the dog comes to you. While it is still a few meters away from you start to praise it (even do so if you have to tug on the leash the whole time).

The goal is to have your dog come back to you without hesitation on your command "Here!" in any situation, whether it is running, sitting, or chasing a living creature. Accordingly, train the dog in various situations.

You call to your dog and your four-legged friend comes, but too slowly for you. If you now correct it, it associates this with coming back, and you achieve the opposite result.

Frequent mistakes with the command "Here!"

Do not use the commands "Come!" and "Here!" for an unpleasant incident. Otherwise, it will always associates these commands with negatives. It is better to get the dog without saying a word.

You give the command "Here!," but stand and wait. The dog looks at you, sees that you are standing there without moving, thinks that you do not want anything after all, and continues to sniff or run around. Instead, squat down or clap your hands and command it to come to you in an encouraging tone of voice.

On the command "Down!" your fellow-lodger should go to the place it normally lies down, or to a place you indicate. If you point out the direction with your hand, you will reinforce your request. At first you will probably have to lead the dog there. Then with one hand carefully pull the legs forward and with the other press on the back of the head until it lies down. Now praise lavishly.

This is how it learns "Down!"

So that it stays "Down!"

To make sure the dog stays down, hold up your hand and give the command "Stay!" while you slowly move away. If it stands up, give the command that you use for what is forbidden at the moment Then, make the dog lie down again by repeating the command "Down!"

Does the dog pull on the leash?

You often see four-legged friends dragging their owner along behind them. This is one of the worst habits an adult dog can have, because it is unpleasant both for the dog and particularly for the owner. Every walk, which should be fun for the dog and owner, turns into a stressful and strenuous cross-country race.

Absolutely break it of the habit of pulling on the leash!

Only a puppy that is getting used to the collar and leash may be allowed to pull on the leash. This gives the puppy a feeling of control over the leash and collar, and it will then accept them more readily. You should break the older dog of the habit of tugging on the leash by using the "Heel!" command.

"Heel!" instead of tugging

This is a more difficult exercise for your fellow-lodger. You must act very consistently here and correct the dog at the right moment. Whenever your four-legged friend pulls on its collar (in any direction), always pull it back immediately (but, please, not with emotionally charged force), give the command "Heel!," and immediately release the tension on the leash.

If you only pull the dog back when it is pulling forward, eventually it will become insensitive to your pressure and will tug even harder. So, bring it back from any direction!

When two strange dogs approach each other, it is normal for them to measure their strength a little and give threat displays. Things get serious, however, when this "game" ends with injuries. A dog that aggressively attacks every other four-legged friend will become not only a terror in the neighborhood but a problem for its owner too. Every time you walk the dog you will tremble when the next dog turns up. Your dog will feel your tension, and will become even more aggressive. The only thing that will help here is a special training program.

Rivalry with other dogs

For the "anti-brawling treatment" you need time and patience — but it pays off. Pick out a walk that the dog is not familiar with and that, if possible, no other dogs use.

This is how to make a brawler gentle

First, let your four-legged friend run off the leash for a while, to give it a good romp. Then, lead it on a short leash, change directions, and give a few commands. If the dog does everything correctly, let it run free as a reward.

Practice obedience

Even when the dog is running free, play with it and keep it occupied, to make it concentrate on you. Later, choose its favorite game. Introduce this game as a ritual, for example, with "Pay attention!" or "Now!," praise it lavishly and give it treats. In this way the game will become some-

Favorite game — the best diversion

thing special for the dog and it will give you its full concentration.

Reenact training situations

When you get the feeling that the initial exercises are working, bring another dog owner into this training program and ask him to approach you with his dog. Now you can test to see if your treatment is already having an effect (on the leash at first). As you pass the other dog, divert your four-legged friend's attention with the afore-mentioned exercises. If it leaves the "enemy" alone, let it run free as a reward. If it becomes fierce again, pull it back with the leash and repeat the exercise until it stays calm.

Test with a free-running dog

After it works on the leash, try the whole thing with the free-running dog. Just before you reach the other dog, divert your dog's attention with its favorite game. It will now prefer this to fighting. If the dog behaves you must of course give it particularly lavish praise. If it still acts aggressively, you must continue practicing on the leash.

Back into the "danger zone"

If your dog no longer gets irritated by the other dog even off the leash, you can risk another trip to the old "danger zone." Important: You must feel calm and confident, or your tension will be transferred to the dog and your efforts will have been wasted.

When you notice that your four-legged friend is again reacting nervously when it sees another dog, in a calm tone of voice immediately give the command "Pay attention!" and start its favorite game.

Has a new dog moved in next door? Have there been barking duals between your pet and the newcomer? On your walks, do you repeatedly meet up with your four-legged friend's "arch enemy," and do the two regularly try to go at each other's throat? Male dogs, in particular, fight over their territory. A "final battle" would establish the pecking order, but you, of course, cannot and do not want this to happen. With clever behavior, however, you can establish a truce.

When several dogs cannot smell one another

Discuss with the owner of the rival dog the routes and times you take walks, so that you no longer meet up with each other.

Avoid the enemy

Divide up the territory. Each owner goes with his four-legged friends on specific paths and avoids the rival's area. If the owners stick to this consistently, their four-legged friends will also get used to it.

Separate paths

You can establish a truce if you and the owner of the other dog choose a meeting place that both dogs are unfamiliar with, where they have no territorial claims. Let the dogs romp about there off the leash. Usually a pecking order will be established during play. Do not, however, trust the peace immediately. In the accustomed territory the four-legged friends could have another falling out.

A meeting in an unfamiliar place

Diversion can also be useful. At the critical places, always have a treat ready for your pet. You should also recommend this to the other owner. In this way the dogs

Diversion creates peace

49

associate the encounter with the rival with a pleasant experience, and the rivalry becomes a minor matter.

Together   Shared walks to settle the rivalry are somewhat nerve-racking at first. In the beginning, walk the animals on short leashes. Later test the behavior of the two dogs on long leashes. Often these shared walks lead to friendship between the two fighting "cocks". Neither dog should be fed until after the walk.

If the four-legged friends growl and threaten each other, it is best to ignore them. Should the two manage to walk side by side sullenly, but calmly, do not praise right away! Only at the conclusion of the walk should you praise the two lavishly.

"Forgetting" the rival   You could also agree with the owner to meet intentionally. Both owners take their four-legged friends on the leash and approach each other. Now it is decisive that they keep the dogs so busy with play or sit-stay exercises, that the four-legged friends "forget" their dislike for each other. If this is successful, praise the animals lavishly and then let them romp around as a reward.

Peaceful at obedience school   If you cannot manage on your own to make your dog peaceful, you should try an obedience school. In this way your four-legged friend will learn to respect other dogs and will finally react more calmly toward other four-legged friends. During the classes the dogs learn that there is only one boss, namely the human being.

Some dogs are as gentle as a lamb and obedient in their own home. As soon as the owner picks up the leash and opens the door, however, they suddenly turn into different dogs. It dashes off, barks at other dogs, chases cyclists, pulls on the leash, and is uncontrollable. You have trained it to act this way, unintentionally of course.

Good at home, wild outside

As a puppy the dog was spoiled. The puppy sleeps less and actively explores its environment, so the owner wants to let it romp around outside. The little one is also encouraged and stimulated with "Go!" and "Run!," to make sure that it rests quietly in its bed when it returns home. For the dog this means: At home I eat and sleep, otherwise, it is boring. Outside is where the action is.

Adventure calls

Take the walk at a different time. If possible, choose a different route, a new collar, and a new leash. This will make the dog more alert. Alternate between going fast and slow and change direction frequently. Do not relax. The dog must conform to your wishes, not you to its.

This is how to break it of the habit of wildness

Combine the free-running phases with playing ball, and always call the dog back. Do not forget to praise it lavishly. In this way the dog will gradually come to understand that it cannot do anything it wants when outside.

Even the most loving animal owner has no choice but to leave his or her fellow-lodger alone at home occasionally. Therefore, it is best to accustom the dog to this early on.

The dog alone at home

TRAINING

First alone in a room

At first, leave the dog alone in a room. In the beginning leave it there for only a few minutes. Gradually increase the amount of time. If it howls and scratches at the door, correct it with a "Bad!"

Play "going away"

Later, put on your coat, explain to the dog briefly that you are going away alone and that it should be good. If it starts to howl or bark right away, go back inside immediately, give the command "Bad!," if necessary shake it briefly by the scruff of the neck, and give the command "Down!" Then quickly go back outside. If it obstinately continues to bark and howl, it is helpful to give the "Bad!" command while holding its muzzle closed for a few minutes.

What does it do while you are gone?

In the beginning, stay outside for only a few minutes, even if the dog does not bark. Quietly go and see what it has been up to in the meantime. If it happens to be jumping out of the bed when you come in, or is in the act of chewing on the rug, you must correct it again with a firm "Bad!" (clap your hands for reinforcement). This will make it believe that you can watch it even when you are not there.

Better not to be angry at all than too late

If, however, you return home after several hours and it has ruined something, correction or punishment is no longer of any use. Although it will "look guilty," because you are mad at it, it will not know why, because it relates the scolding only to the present.

Repeat the absence exercises, and stay away a little longer each time, until your dog has gotten accustomed to it. Nevertheless, you must not leave it alone too much for this reason: Dogs need the company of human beings. Loneliness causes them much suffering.

For a short time you can leave the radio or cassette player on, to keep your pet from feeling so lonely. If you have a yard and your companion can move around in it freely and can watch what is going on around it, is also not as bad as being locked alone inside the house. Make sure that it does not bark constantly, or can escape through the fence.

Music and the yard as pastimes

But even the yard is no substitute for attention. You must give your dog more attention when you return home after a fairly long absence.

BAD HABITS

Begging? No, thanks! Begging at the table is a bad habit that you should not allow to develop in the first place. Many visitors that are invited to dinner feel disturbed by begging four-legged friends. Some people are moved by the imploring look. Some dogs even become so bold as to steal food from the plate, which also is very unhygienic.

What tastes good to humans can harm the dog Anyone who raises his four-legged friend to be a beggar is not doing the animal a favor either. Foods meant for humans, including salty foods, spicy foods, or sweets, are often hard for the dog's stomach to digest and can cause health problems and obesity.

The dog has no business at the table You should always give the dog its food in its own place, only in its dish. If possible always at the same time. Never give it scraps from the table.

Ignore or a lemon You must sternly ignore grins, sad looks, and unseemly behavior until the dog stops begging. If it becomes too annoying, send it to its place or put it in another room. You can also offer it a slice of lemon each time it begs. This will quickly break it of this bad habit.

Ask your guests not to offer the dog any morsels, because this will also make it prone to stealing. It must not receive and accept food from strangers at all, for the sake of its own safety alone (poisoning). **No morsels from strangers**

When puppies playfully snap at your hand, or at other people, it seems harmless. Nevertheless, you should not let it happen. This is how the puppy tests the pecking order. To break it of this habit, hold it by the cheeks for about a minute when it tries to snap at you. After two or three tries, your four-legged friend will stop doing it. **The puppy snaps at people**

In general, we must say that dogs express their mood through barking and, by doing so, are trying to defend "their territory." If a dog barks and bays constantly, it can get on people's nerves — particularly those of passers-by and neighbors, who then develop a dislike for or even become infuriated with the dog. **Persistent barking gets on the nerves**

As soon as it starts barking for no reason, give a sharp command of "Out!," until it understands that it cannot bark at everything and everybody, and learns to distinguish between what is important and what is not. **It must be able to distinguish between what is important and what is not**

If scolding is not effective, you must employ more intensive measures. When it barks, give the command "Out!," grab its muzzle from above, and hold it closed for several minutes. This "biting over the muzzle" has also been observed in wolves. Mother wolves use it to correct their young when they howl.

The dog jumps up on you

As a sign of greeting and joy, dogs often jump up on their owner. If you want to stop this, push it away and give the command "Bad!" You must, however, be consistent. If it is usually allowed to jump, but not when you are dressed up, you will only confuse it.

Keep away from the litter box

Some dogs are "drawn" by litter boxes, the contents of which they eat. If you notice this vice with your dog, it is best to put the litter box in the bathroom.

Hammer a small nail into the door frame, and tie the nail to the door handle with a string. The cracked door should be just wide enough for your cat, but not your dog, to get through.

If the dog is as small as the cat or smaller, put a board in front of the door, so that the cat can jump over it, but the dog cannot.

Another possibility is to put the litter box in the bathtub. This is no problem for the cat, but a small dog cannot get in.

The dog runs away

Stray dogs are in danger of being run over, stolen, shot, or poisoned. It is not easy to break the dog of the habit of running away. Consider what the cause could be. Examples: too little affection, loneliness, too few walks, mistreatment, etc.

To break the dog of the habit of running away, you must pay more attention to it and teach it that it must not leave the yard without you. You can only do this if you catch it in the act of escaping. A loud command of "Bad!" is appropriate. You can scare it by rattling a can with coins inside it.

Catch it in the act

Then call it back in a friendly tone of voice and praise it when it comes. Were you to scold it now, it would think that coming back is the bad habit.

By nature, dogs are prone to chase anything that moves. When the hunting instinct is so pronounced that it chases everything from rabbits to cyclists, you must put a stop to this as soon as possible. Do not, however, try it with hysterical screaming. This will achieve exactly the opposite result. Your agitated voice will only excite it to chase even more.

When the dog chases anything that moves

Put the dog on a leash about 10 meters long, and let it walk on a slack leash. As soon as an "object" gets its attention and it tries to rush away, pull it back with a sharp tug. This will teach the dog that as soon as it chases, there will be unpleasant consequences. If the leash method does not work after some time, try it in conjunction with the rattling can.

This is how to stop the chaser

BEHAVIOR

Fear in the dog

Dogs usually become afraid when the owner leaves them at home. Often, however, there are situations that have caused the dog pain or frightened it. This can lead to anxiety.

Fear as protection

We should not look at fear as just a negative. It even has a natural protective function and saves the dog from dangers and sometimes can even save the animal's life. Puppies first exhibit fear at an age of approximately seven weeks. This is completely natural. We must consider only excessive fear as aberrant behavior.

Fear can be reduced

If the dog is shy and timid because of bad experiences, it is possible to win the animal's trust and to reduce its fear. To do this, however, you need patience and the ability to empathize. The dog must repeatedly experience situations that it particularly fears as nonthreatening or pleasant.

Brave second dog

Sometimes it is also helpful to add a second, more self-confident dog, so that the "scaredy-cat" feels more secure in time. This is only true, however, when the newcomer is good-natured and peaceful. Otherwise, it will have the totally opposite effect.

When your dog makes itself very stiff and raises the hair on its back when it encounters another dog, this is not necessarily a sign of an impending fight, but, rather, can signal its fear. Fear of other dogs usually occurs when the four-legged friend has previously been bitten, or has had other bad experiences with others of its kind. After such an experience, you should let the fellow-lodger play with a well-behaved, gentle dog as soon as possible. It would be wrong to isolate the dog, because this would only increase its fear of other dogs.

Fear of rivals

Some dogs snap at people for no reason. These dogs are so-called "fear biters." They do not bite out of aggression, but because they fear something bad and want to forestall this threat. Here, too, much patience and attention are required. You must show the dog repeatedly that it has nothing to fear in specific situations.

Dogs that bite out of fear

Most dogs like to ride in the car. It can happen, however, that some four-legged friends also develop a downright fear of cars. Maybe they have gotten very sick on some occasion, or they have had some other unpleasant experience. The sound of the engine could also upset them.

Fear in the car

The best way to approach this problem is to make the dog feel at home first in the parked car. Later, you can start the car, but do not drive away immediately. Instead, pet your dog and speak reassuringly to it.

First, get the dog used to the parked car

Break down fear step by step

Lengthen the trips gradually. The first trip should be short. Ask someone to sit with your four-legged friend and pet it during the trip. When it understands that nothing bad will happen to it in the car, it will finally overcome its fear.

Fear of noise

If your dog becomes frightened by loud sounds and noise and possibly even runs away, accustom it to noise step by step.

- Clatter with the spoon when you put the food in the dish.
- Play loudly with the dog.
- During a thunderstorm, keep the dog near you in the house and handle and pet it in a relaxed and cheerful manner. The dog will also detect your uneasiness.
- In another room, drop an object noisily to the floor. When the dog arrives and examines it inquisitively, praise it in a cheerful tone of voice.
  Never leave it at home alone when fireworks are going off nearby. Stay with it and speak to it in a soothing tone of voice.

Fear of objects

Some dogs stop abruptly in front of objects (garbage can, unusually large vehicle, and so forth) and cannot be made to walk past it, or they try to backtrack. Laugh cheerfully, touch the object, so that the dog sees that nothing will happen. When it moves closer, praise it.

Fear of humans

If your puppy is afraid of someone, ask the person simply to ignore the dog. Move as close to the person as possible, hold a relaxed conversation, and carefully pull the dog a little closer. Instruct the person to crouch down a short distance from the dog.

Timid dogs find it more agreeable when they can approach you. Therefore, do not go to the dog, reach out to it, or stare it directly in the eyes. On principle, dogs dislike this! Instead, talk to it in a friendly tone of voice, and then take it by the collar and stroke its chest. If things do not work out with a single lesson, arrange further encounters for practice.

Some people are physically and psychologically unable to assume the role of leader in relation to the dog. They have neglected (maybe because the puppy was so sweet?) to train the dog in time, and to show it its place in the pecking order (without hitting and yelling!). By its nature, however, the dog expects to assume a set position in the hierarchy. If you do not show the dog its place, it tries to take things into its own hands by assuming the position of "boss." This can (naturally, this varies from breed to breed) go so far that the dog, because of dominance behavior, will even become aggressive toward its owner and growl or even snap at him. With consistency and without force you can "change its mind" as follows:

When the dog gains the upper hand

Give your four-legged friend neither food nor attention for a day, and if possible avoid situations in which it is aggressive toward you. Act as if it is not even there,

No food, no contact

except when you give it a command. If the dog now comes to you on its own and wants your attention, give it the command "Sit!" or "Down!" If it obeys, pet it and give it part of its food ration. Repeat the lesson several more times and on several more days, and give more and more commands.

You must not do an "about-face"

The purpose of the aforementioned exercise is to make the dog understand that you have the authority. Of decisive importance for success is that you do not do an "about-face" and cause the pecking order to be reversed again, or you will have wasted your effort. Furthermore, all family members must play along. This means that nobody else may undo the lesson by giving the dog treats and sympathy or attention.

Play and sport

Puppies need about as much attention as children for them to develop properly. Play is a wonderful form of attention for the dog and is also helpful for training. Moreover, the puppy learns a great deal during play while it is still with its mother and siblings — it is, so to speak, a form of training. Generally speaking, young dogs should have frequent opportunities to play with others of their kind (grass play area, obedience classes for puppies). Adult dogs also need to play. In so doing they strengthen the bond with their owner. With a game you can compensate your four-legged friend for having had to spend the day alone, or distract it in a problem situation.

Puppies need much variety and are constantly driven by curiosity. They have to examine anything new and will immediately drop whatever they are doing to investigate something else. Therefore, you should be imaginative with play and frequently give the puppy new toys. Make sure, however, that you use things that are suitable for dogs. Older dogs busy themselves more intensively with an object and no longer need as much variety.

Young and inquisitive

During play the four-legged friend can also work off suppressed and pent-up need to hunt and attack. If it has no opportunity to do so, it will seek out substitute prey. It will chase anything that plays or moves: children, cats, cyclists . . .

Substitute prey from lack of exercise

The toy must not be made of a dangerous material or be so small that the dog could swallow it. Plastic and soft rubber are not suitable. Plastic can shatter and hurt the dog, and with soft rubber parts, it could bite a piece off and swallow it. Nylabones® and Gumabones® are ideal and available at pet shops.

Only have toys that are suitable for dogs

The dog exhibits the typical invitation to play when it rests on its front legs (the trunk touches the ground, to emphasize that it has no intention of attacking), and raises its hindquarters. At the same time it makes short "hops," as if it were trying to say, "Let's go!"

Come and play with me!

Come and run away
• The dog happily runs up to you and drops

Games

the ball or stick at your feet. As soon as you reach for it, it snatches the object again and dashes off.

Playing fetch
- The dog brings you an object, waits for you to throw it, and then chases it.

Running around in a circle
- When the dog is particularly boisterous, it likes to run in a circle around its "master" or "mistress."

Tag
- Games of tag are highly popular with dogs as well as children. The dog also likes to "capture" its owner (in so doing it will try to "bite" you on the ankle, as it learned while playing with its mother) or allow itself to be caught by its owner.

The dog, a soccer fan
- You do not need a goal to play soccer. In the duel with the owner for a ball (dribble the ball ahead of you), the four-legged friend will turn out to be a "strong opponent."

Who is stronger?
- Wrestle and tussle with your four-legged friend. If it gets too boisterous and bites a little too hard, make a clear sound and give it the command "Out!" This will teach it to do its play biting "gently." Make sure, however, that you do not allow puppies to snap at every hand even when you are not playing with them!

Catching objects on the fly
- The dog runs to catch light objects you throw to it in the air. The Nylabone Frisbees® are well suited for this purpose.

The "fight" for a prize

- Wrestle with your dog over a prize. This could be an old glove, a heavy rag, or a stick, but never the leash. Otherwise, it will always view it as substitute prey and a toy. Then you will have problems when you try to walk the dog on the leash again.

All dogs are fascinated by the "prize fighting game." When they tug on the object, growl, and finally run off with the "prize," they can effectively work off aggression and their hunting instinct. To avoid threatening the pecking order, it is important that you end up the winner in this game!

Work off aggression

Any kind of running is a lot of fun for your dog: obstacle racing, cross-country running, and running alongside the bicycle (but only if the dog is obedient and you do not ride too fast, to avoid overtaxing your four-legged friend).

Over hedge and ditch

Agility is a sport in which the dog learns to overcome different obstacles (information is available from obedience schools), which is great fun for the master or mistress and the dog. Both the dog and the human being get plenty of exercise, which is healthy for the two of them.

Agility sport for active dogs

The owner runs the course with the dog, gives it commands for the respective obstacle, and offers encouragement. You must have patience, endurance, and bring dog treats to achieve good performance. Your companion needs curiosity, courage, and a strong bond to you.

The owner runs alongside

Each obstacle is a challenge

The four-legged friends jump through tires, negotiate a slalom course, crawl through a tunnel, climb a sloping wall, jump over a wooden wall, and much more. Each time the dog successfully masters an obstacle, you must bestow lavish praise. After the dog gains experience, it runs the course against the clock.

Only if the dog wants to

Do not force your dog to engage in agility out of your own ambition, if it does not enjoy it at all or is not suited for breed-specific reasons.

Is your dog talented?

Basically, all lively, playful, healthy dogs are suited for this sport. They like to be kept busy and to do something with their favorite person. Very large, placid, lazy four-legged friends are, of course, less suited. During training you will at least have to skip the jumps.

"Toys" also take part

Even small dogs can take part and often do well because they are so lively. They compete on a second course, with smaller, lower obstacles.

Basic training is a prere-quisite

If you want to be competitive in agility sport, you must give your dog basic obedience training, because it must obey your commands to the letter. In agility training, the four-legged friend also learns to react to hand signals.

When can you begin?

You can already start at home with a few exercises when the dog is four or five months old, such as crawling through a tunnel or running a slalom between poles.

You may not yet begin with jumping exercises with such young animals, because they could suffer injury to the shoulder apparatus (you can begin jumping exercises starting at about a year).

Another prerequisite for agility is that you have previously occupied yourself and played much with your companion, and have already begun to train the dog with patience and consistency. In basic obedience training, the owner is also taught how to teach properly. The training of both the dog and its master is the foundation of agility.

Owner and dog— a close team

Older dogs may also take part, as long as they do not have problems with their vertebrae, joints or breathing.

VACATION

Better leash than grief

To spare you from grief, anger, and quarreling, you should keep your four-legged companion on the leash in the woods. Take the longest possible leash, to give the dog the feeling of still being able to run around. In any case, you must obey the leash laws in areas where they apply.

The dog as vacation companion

Dogs, unlike cats, are ideal vacation companions. No matter where you go, the only important thing to the dog is to be with its owner or "family pack." This will make it happy. On vacation you also have time to give your companion plenty of attention. To make sure that everything goes smoothly, you should start planning in time.

Dogs welcome

There are many hotels, motels, and campgrounds, both domestic and foreign, where dogs are welcome. Even on some beaches, no one will complain about your dog, as long as it is obedient and does not bother anyone. Make sure that the dog does not relieve itself where other guests go sunbathing.

Have animal-friendly hotels and motels or travel agencies provide written confirmation of the agreement. Tell them the breed and size of the dog, and ask about the hotel's conditions.

Is the hotel really dog-friendly?

Inquire whether your dog liability insurance also covers damage in hotels or covers travel at all (obtain written confirmation).

What will your insurance pay?

Definitely inquire about the legal entry regulations for pets. You can obtain information from the respective consulate, veterinarians, and tour organizers. Some countries (for example, Great Britain) have very long quarantine periods (six months and more), so that it is no longer possible to bring your pet along.

Trips abroad

Do not rely on entry information from the previous year. The regulations very often change within a short time! It is best to make inquiries before each trip.

In any case, your four-legged friend must be vaccinated against rabies on all trips abroad. The dog must have been vaccinated within the last year, and at least a month before departure.

A rabies vacci-nation is always necessary

You must not put off vaccinations until the last minute. The immune system of the animal needs a certain amount of time to produce sufficient antibodies following a vaccination to be able to effectively ward off disease. Preventive vaccinations for distemper — as with

Get vacci-nations in time

rabies — should be given at least four weeks before the trip.

Have you made all preparations?

The following list will help you to start your vacation well prepared:

- Inquire about entry regulations
- Inquire about travel conditions with the railroad line or airline
- Plan the journey so that not too much is not expected of the dog (changeovers, the opportunity to eat and drink water, and so forth)
- Vaccinations, checkups: have vaccination and health certificates issued
- Muzzle, leash, collar (name and address tag!)
- Medications for vomiting and diarrhea, travel sickness, and regular daily health.
- Drinking water for on the way, food and water dishes
- Commercial dog food (do not forget the can opener and spoon)
- Sleeping basket or blanket
- Brushes, possibly shampoo
- Scoop and bags for disposing of feces

Bring enough food!

Bring a large enough supply of the kind of food your dog is used to. In this way, you will avoid the possibility of the dog not tolerating or being unable to get used to strange food.

The dog in the car

Most dogs like to travel in the car, if they have become accustomed to it in time. The dog should associate the car with a positive experience. Therefore, do not only take the dog in the car to bring it to the veterinarian. Start with a few short trips.

If your pet is not an enthusiastic car traveler, the following can be helpful:

- The dog should lie down or sit so that if possible it cannot see what is going by outside. A passenger who distracts it, holds its head in his or her lap and pets it is ideal.
- Drive smoothly, take curves more slowly than usual, and brake carefully.
- Vent fresh air into the car and avoid smoking.
- Talk soothingly to the dog, to make it feel safe.

Your dog does not like car trips?

Before longer trips, the veterinarian can prescribe a mild sedative. Please do not administer medications that are meant for humans. Human medications affect animals differently.

The proper place for your dog is the back seat. If you always assign it to the same place with its own blanket, later it will sit there on its own. Restless animals that climb around endanger the driver. They could also be frightened by a noise or an unexpected situation and be thrown into a panic. Lively four-legged friends should be kept on a short enough leash that they cannot jump from their seat.

Four-legged friends belong in the back seat

On longer trips do not feed your dog beforehand, and feed it only a little to make it less likely to vomit. It can safely get by without food for a day.

Starvation diet for travel sickness

Do not forget to bring its water dish and enough water. It can survive for a fairly long time without food, but it must have enough water.

Make occas-ional stops

Consider that your dog must relieve itself about four times a day. Furthermore, particularly if it is a dog that likes to run, it needs its exercise. Stop frequently and run around with the dog. This is also good for you after sitting for a long time!

Roasting in the heat?

If you must leave the dog in the car for a while, do not park in the blazing sun. Also, consider how the sun travels during the day. Windows opened a crack do not provide the dog with enough to stay cool and to breathe. There is the danger that it could suffocate. Consider how you would feel if you had to spend a fairly long time in the blazing sun without being able to open the windows!

The dog may not come along?

If you cannot bring your dog with you, it is best to board it with relatives or friends, who know it well and that it really likes. Let the trusted person(s) come along on walks and take the dog on the leash a few times before the trip.

The master returns

Before a longer trip, give your pet to the entrusted person a few times for short periods. This will show the four-legged friend that you will return for it.

Ease the pain of separation

Discuss with the entrusted person all peculiarities and habits of the dog, feeding and walking times, and give them enough food. The dog's customary sleeping basket or its mattress, and a few familiar toys will ease the pain of separation. Also, provide a piece of clothing with your scent on it. In addition, you should leave the vaccination certificates and money in case a visit to the veterinarian proves necessary.

If you have absolutely no other choice, you can also board your four-legged friend in a dog kennel. You must, however, inspect it thoroughly beforehand to make sure that your dog will be treated well. It is best to write down the dog's peculiarities and habits, and to discuss everything in detail with the staff.

Dog kennel

Dogs should be expected to take a longer flight only when it is absolutely necessary. It is a great strain on the animal, particularly when it has to stay alone in the cargo hold. On charter flights, dogs are rarely allowed to come along. Book your flight as early as possible, because only a limited number of four-legged friends may be permitted to come along.

Dogs on the airplane

Smaller dogs up to 11 or 18 pounds (inquire with the airline) may be transported in the passenger compartment in a securely locked pet carrier. Larger dogs must travel in the pressurized cargo hold. It is advisable to administer a sedative prescribed by the veterinarian to the dog before the flight.

Small dogs may travel in the passenger compartment

On international flights, the flight attendants will care for the dog and provide it

Flight attendants

with food and water. Also discuss this with the airline.

Dogs on the train With most dogs you can also travel by train without any problems. They must, however, be muzzled and kept on a leash. You will have to pay half-fare for the dog. Small four-legged friends may travel for free as, so to speak, carry-on luggage in a bag or small pet carrier. Do not forget to bring a can of food, water, and a water dish for your pet.

Use a longer stop to walk the dog. This allows the dog to get a little exercise and relieve itself.

Sleeping car permitted The dog may be permitted in the sleeping car, but only when you book the compartment for yourself alone.

Dog ahoy! Dogs are allowed to travel with you on many cruise ships. Sometimes there is even a separate dog service. Inquire whether four-legged friends are allowed to stay in the cabin. It can also be the case that the dog is allowed on the ship, but must stay in a separate section in the kennel. Then you should consider if you should even bring the dog along, because the trip certainly would not be fun for your animal. Dogs are not allowed on some cruise ships. Inquire ahead of time with the cruise line or the travel agency.

DOGS AND CATS

Basically, yes. There are very few exceptions where the dog and cat cannot get used to each other at all. It is frequently the case that cats and dogs become close friends and even sleep snuggled together in the dog's bed. The cat, in particular, seeks out the warmth.

Can you keep dogs and cats together?

Misunderstandings can occur, at least in the beginning, because the dog and cat have different, in some cases even opposing, behavior patterns for expressing something, to put it mildly.

Why misunderstandings occur

Breeds with a stronger hunting instinct, such as terriers, which once were bred exclusively as hunters, find it more difficult to get along with cats than do herding or working dogs.

"Hunters" find it harder to adjust

Puppies and kittens naturally get accustomed to each other with the fewest problems. An adult cat or an adult dog also accepts the other best in the juvenile stage. A puppy that has become acquainted with cats at a very early age will no longer view them as prey throughout its life.

Less of a problem: young animals

DOGS AND CATS

Cautious approach

Proceed cautiously and very calmly with the first encounter between your pet and the new fellow-lodger. The new pet should stay in one room at first. Your "old" friend should have the opportunity to approach and see the newcomer first. Do not put the two four-legged friends face to face. This leads to tension, fear, or aggression.

Do not leave unsupervised

Do not leave the two unsupervised in the beginning. A temporary quiet does not necessarily mean that the fronts have been settled. Watch for agitation, fear, or threat displays with the four-legged friends. It is best to distract them with food. Put the dog and cat in the same room, but far apart. In this way the two are distracted, but still smell the other and associate with each other the pleasant act of eating. You must expect it to take a few weeks for the four-legged friends to get used to each other.

Accustom them to each other in their sleep

Put something that smells of the cat in the dog's sleeping place and vice versa. In this way, the two animals will, so to speak, get used to each other in their sleep, without "something happening" in the process.

Are large dogs more dangerous?

No matter how big the dog is, by nature the cat assumes the position of "boss" — as it, of course, also ultimately does in relation to the owner. In this respect, size is not of decisive importance. Only very rarely does this pecking order not become established. Should this happen, large dogs are, of course, more dangerous.

Cats usually threaten dogs by raising their hair and hissing. Occasionally they also slap the dog a few times. This in itself is not serious. The situation becomes troublesome only when the cat is frightened and timid and runs away. This automatically triggers the dog's hunting instinct, which could cause it to bite the cat.

What can happen?

Watch your four-legged friends closely. When the dog wags its tail amiably and the cat invites the dog to romp around with play gestures, the spell is broken and the friendship sealed. This takes a while, because the cat does not know right away what the tail wagging means. It shows it somewhat differently: It gently bites the dog's tail, which the dog also must get used to.

When have they made friends?

Even when the dog and cat tolerate each other and even sleep together, jealousy and fighting can be triggered when food is the topic. Moreover, the dog and cat have different nutritional needs and should not eat the other's food.

Shared "bed," separate "table"

Last but not least, the dog and cat differ in their eating behavior. The dog as a pack animal quickly gulps its food. Cats as solitary animals do not need to do this. They eat slowly and do not eat everything at one sitting. Therefore, it is better to feed the dog and cat separately.

The dog tries to be friendly, the cat misinterprets its gesture as a threat — and vice versa. This is the reason for many misun-

Body language

derstandings. In their life together the two must first learn the other's "foreign language."

Raised tail

- Beware, I am big and strong, approach me submissively, says the dog, when it raises its tail. The cat, on the other hand, shows that it is in a friendly mood and wants to be petted.

Raised paws

- I want your attention, play with me, the dog is trying to say, when it lifts its paw slightly (be nice to me, when it raises them). Beware when the cat lifts its paw, because it is preparing to take a swipe.

"Bowing"

- I want to play with you, signals the dog when it "bows" (presses its upper body to the floor and stretches its paws forward). This gesture means exactly the opposite with the cat: it shows that it wants to be left alone now.

Lying on its back

- A dog presents its throat and belly to its opponent when it "gives up" and lies on its back. The cat assumes the supine position when it feels threatened, and in this way reveals its weapons — the sharp claws.

Staring

- Cats stare at the other cat, because it is customary among cats to make contact in this way and through particular looks to signal if they have good intentions. Among dogs it is not customary to stare at others, because this is more likely to make the four-legged friend aggressive.

Can the dog and cat infect each other with diseases?

There are only a few diseases that can be transmitted from the dog to the cat and vice versa.

Ear mites

- Cats are rather insensitive to ear mites, and for a long time exhibit hardly any symptoms when they are infected. They can infect the dog, however, which then exhibits severe symptoms of illness. With ear mites, the cat therefore must always receive treatment too, or it will infect the dog again.

Scabies

- This condition can also be transmitted between dogs and cats and vice versa. Always treat both.

Tapeworms, salmonella

- Tapeworms, such as the pumpkinseed-like canine tapeworm, and certain bacteria, such as salmonella, can also be transmitted between the four-legged friends. The dog and cat must always be dewormed at the same time!

Fleas

- These parasites also jump from dog to cat, and vice versa!

Feline parvovirus

- There still exists misunderstanding about parvovirus, because it is also called feline parvovirus of dogs. The dog cannot be infected with this virus by the cat, however, and the cat not from the dog. There is misunderstanding because both pathogens belong to the same group of viruses, namely the parvoviruses.

GROOMING

Coat care   A shiny coat is a visible sign of the health and vitality of the dog. The type of coat care depends on whether you have a long-haired, short-haired, or rough-haired dog. No matter what kind of dog you have, take the time for daily brushing. This simultaneously has several pluses: it is absolutely necessary for the care of the coat, the dog enjoys the extra attention, and it helps you to keep the house clean, because in the process you remove dust and dead hair.

The care of the short haired dog   The short-haired dog also welcomes its daily quarter hour of brushing. You will need a brush with stiff bristles and a nubbly rubber brush. First, brush with the stiff-bristled brush vigorously against the grain, that is, from back to front. In this way you brush out the dead hair. Next, take the nubbly rubber brush and brush the dog with the grain from head to tail and from back to belly. Finally, wipe with a damp chamois cloth or bath towel over the coat with the grain. This removes the remaining dust and produces a shiny coat.

At the time when the coat is shed, run your hand through the dog's coat against the grain before brushing. This loosens the dead hair and the undercoat and brings them to the surface, where you can brush them out easily. This is important, because dead hair can cause intense itching.

With the long-haired dog, the daily brushing is of special benefit. Brush the dog with a brush with long bristles or a soft wire brush edged with natural bristles. For the long-haired dog you also need a comb to remove mats from the coat. Important: the comb must have coarse, widely spaced, rounded teeth, because a fine-toothed comb would also pull out healthy hair. With the long-haired dog, also wipe the coat with a damp chamois cloth at the end.

The care of the long-haired dog

With the rough-haired dog, use a wire brush with bent wire teeth and brush it in the same directions as described with the short-haired dog. Besides the daily brushing, the rough-haired dog must be plucked twice a year.

The care of the rough-haired dog

Plucking is not painful for the dog if it is done at the right time, that is, when the dog starts to shed. Were you not to pluck the dog, it would scratch itself constantly to remove the itchy, dead hair.

Does plucking hurt?

Stripping knives are used to pluck the mature hair. Plucking thus speeds up hair replacement. Because the growth rate of the hair varies between individual dogs, the intervals between plucking also vary.

What happens during plucking?

Can you pluck the dog yourself?

It is better to have an expert pluck the dog. If you absolutely insist on plucking your dog yourself, you should get help at first from a skilled breeder to avoid disfiguring the dog. In any case, begin with its back, from the back of the head to the tail. The dog must be seated. Then, stand the dog up and pluck the sides of the body. Finally, work carefully over the sensitive parts of the body, such as the head, ears, and throat.

Clipping and cutting the coat

Poodles must be clipped at six-week intervals to maintain a neat appearance. You can choose whether you prefer to see your pet in the classic standard clip or in the pet clip. The pet retains more of the coat, so it offers greater protection against cold. It is therefore particularly recommended for small and toy pets.

You must clip Kerry Blue Terriers and Bedlington Terriers with the clipping machine. Carefully use with the clippers over the comb to maintain their typical appearance.

The hair around the eyes

With some dogs (for example, spaniels and terriers), excessively long hairs around the eyes irritate the conjunctiva and cornea, and cause a sticky discharge from the eyes. In this case, trim the hairs in question carefully with blunt scissors.

Forehead fringes

With some dog breeds, such as the Maltese, a head with long and thick hair is required for shows. If you do not show these dogs, however, you can safely improve their vision by trimming the hair away from the eyes.

Trim long hair between the foot pads to prevent them from becoming matted. Another benefit is that the dog will track less dirt into the house.

The hair between the foot pads

For reasons of hygiene it is sometimes necessary to trim the hair around the penis and vulva — for example, when hairs get stuck together by a discharge from an inflammation of the foreskin.

Hair around the genitals

Never trim the sensitive sensory hairs on the dog's muzzle.

Whiskers

Of course, you may bathe dogs, but not too often. With most dogs, four baths a year are sufficient. The dog does not have a sweaty coat, because it has sweat glands only on the foot pads. The dog's skin, however, has sebaceous glands in the skin, which uniformly oil the skin and coat. This oil does an excellent job of protecting the dog against cold and moisture. The oily film makes the coat water-repellent. This is why the dog only needs to shake itself a few times after swimming to be dry again. If you bathe the dog too often, it loses this oily film and is more susceptible to colds and skin diseases. Dust and dirt also collect much more quickly when the coat is too dry.

May you bathe dogs

If the dog has rolled in dirt and excrement, a bath is absolutely necessary. Run warm water (35 to 38° C) into the bathtub. The bath water should only be belly deep to the standing dog. To keep the dog from slipping, use a non-slip rubber mat. For cleaning use exclusively alkali-free dog shampoo. You should use medicinal bath salts only after consulting your veterinarian. Make sure that no water gets in the ears. The best way to avoid this is to plug the ear canals with cotton wool before the bath. Do not let the dog drink the bath water, because the soap in it could cause an upset stomach. When rinsing, make sure that lather does not get in the dog's eyes.

You must dry the dog well after the bath, to keep it from catching cold. If you want to use a hair drier to dry the coat, you should accustom the dog to the hair drier even before the first bath. You can also rub the dog down thoroughly with a big bath towel. In cold weather you should be especially cautious: Even when the animal appears to be dry, it still remains sensitive to cold for a fairly long time. Therefore, you must wait a few hours before you go outside with it. If possible bathe the dog after the evening walk, so that it can stay inside the house until following day.

May you bathe very young puppies? With very young dogs the danger of catching a cold is naturally greater than with fully grown dogs. Puppies that are younger than 12 weeks old may not be bathed. Puppies that are older than 12 weeks and have already had their shots can be bathed if necessary. Dry the puppy particularly thoroughly and make sure that it is not exposed to draft.

Most dogs require regular nail care.

Nail care

With dogs that get too little exercise or exercise only on soft surfaces, the nails do not wear down as fast as they grow. Ideally, the tip of the nail should be level with the foot pads. If the nails are longer, the foot mechanism suffers. To prevent this from happening, you must clip them. You can also recognize excessively long nails by the dog's "loud footsteps." The dew claws must be clipped regularly. Because they do not touch the ground, they do not wear down and readily become ingrown. This is very painful and often leads to abscesses.

When must you clip the nails?

If possible, you should leave this to the expert — a breeder or veterinarian. The nails should only be clipped with a special nail clipper, because it does not crush the nail, but cuts the nail diagonally from the front without hurting the dog. You also must not clip the nails too short, to keep them from bleeding. With light-colored nails you can see where the blood vessels begin, but not with dark-colored nails. Therefore, you should clip dark nails only a little each time, but clip them more frequently.

Is it hard to clip the nails?

If the dog has very hard, brittle nails, you should soak the paws for ten minutes in warm, soapy water before clipping the nails. To prevent brittle nails, you should rub olive oil on them from time to time.

Hard, brittle nails

Yes, tooth care is very important! The story is the same here as well: an ounce of prevention is better than a pound of cure.

Tooth care

Through strict oral hygiene, the dog, too, can retain sparkling white, healthy teeth for many years.

Brushing the teeth

It is best to accustom the puppy to having its teeth brushed daily. Use one of the toothpastes for dogs available on the market, because they taste good to the dog and it is safe to swallow them. Use a special toothbrush for dogs. Particularly practical are the brushes that you can simply slide over your finger. If your dog absolutely does not tolerate having its teeth cleaned with toothpaste and toothbrush, try to clean its teeth in the traditional way: wrap your index finger in a damp cloth dipped in whiting and use it carefully to clean the dog's teeth and gums.

Self-cleaning of the teeth

Intense chewing — such as Nylabone®, Gumabones® or Plaque Attackers® — promotes the self-cleaning of the teeth and prevents the formation of tartar.

Tartar

Tartar is dangerous for the teeth. It is a first-class carrier of bacteria and causes bad breath, cavities, and gingivitis. It also leads to the loosening and loss of the teeth. Furthermore, it can cause painful inflammations of the gums. The gums can get so painful that finally the animal refuses to eat at all. Therefore, the tartar absolutely must be removed at least once a year. This is a routine procedure for the veterinarian. The dog is given a mild anesthetic, and the procedure is soon completed with ultrasound without damaging the tooth enamel.

The care of the eyes is limited to wiping the eye with a damp linen cloth. Always wipe from the outside in, that is, from the outside corner of the eye in toward the nose. This procedure also removes light encrustations in the corner of the eye. Do not use a wad of cotton wool or a paper towel to clean the eye, because the dog could get fibers in its eyes.

The morning eye care

Important: Never poke around in the ear canal with a cotton swab, because a healthy dog's ear cleans itself, and an infected ear requires veterinary treatment. Clean only the inside of the external ear with a cloth dunked in water or olive oil. If too much hair is growing in the ear opening that the ear canal no longer receives sufficient ventilation, you must pluck the hairs.

Be careful with the ears!

THE SEASONS

Spring

As far as weather is concerned, the spring presents hardly any problems for dogs. Precisely the mild spring weather, however, induces many owners to overtax their untrained dogs on excessively long spring walks. Particularly with older dogs, it is advisable to have the veterinarian check the heart and circulation before pleasant weather arrives. The veterinarian can then prescribe, if necessary, medication to strengthen the heart and circulation. The spring is also ideally suited for performing planned operations, such as neutering. Wounds heal particularly well in the spring.

Summer

Sweating: When dogs sweat, they pant. The reason for this is that the dog cannot sweat over its whole body as we humans can, but rather only on the paws. This is not sufficient, however, for regulating the body temperature in the summer heat. The result: The dog must pant.

Panting: When the dog pants, it takes 130 to 140 very rapid and shallow breaths per minute. Normally, it breathes 10 to 40 times a minute. Thus, the dog sweats to a certain degree through its tongue. This means that it primarily breathes through the nose, where the air picks up moisture from the nasal mucous membrane. Finally, it expels the water-saturated air back out through the mouth. In this way the dog evaporates up to 200 grams of water per hour. Therefore, always offer sufficient drinking water. It is best to set out several water dishes in the house and yard.

If you do not pay attention, your four-legged companion could easily fall victim to heatstroke.

Heat

Dogs that are locked in cars are in extreme danger. Even if the windows are opened a crack, the temperature in the car can rise to as much as 70° C. In particular danger are dogs with a very dense coat and the "brachycephalic" dog breeds (Boxer, Bulldog, Pugs, Pekingese, and so forth). These breeds namely have a short muzzle, an elongated soft palate, and make snoring sounds when they breathe. They are particularly susceptible to heatstroke. Make sure that you park your car in the shade and open the windows wide enough that the air can circulate. Do not leave the dog

Heat–stroke in the car

for more than a few minutes—better safe than sorry.

Should long-haired dogs be clipped in the summer?

Dogs with a thick undercoat — such as the Old English Sheepdog, Shetland Sheepdog, and some mixed-breeds — certainly get relief when they are clipped in the summer. With dog breeds that are regularly plucked or clipped, this, of course, should not be neglected in the summer. Long-haired dogs with little undercoat and a long, silky coat should not be clipped.

The dog in the swimming pool

The dog can also easily suffer a heatstroke by the swimming pool or at the beach if it must roast in the blazing sun alongside its master or mistress. At least set up a sunshade, and provide fresh drinking water. If the dog wants to go in the water, you can let it swim without worrying. Diving does not harm the dog either, as long as it does so willingly. When it leaves the water, rub it dry with a towel, so that it does not spray other bathers when it shakes itself.

Swimming

You must never force your dog to go in the water. The dog could panic and even drown.

Draft in the car

When you drive with your dog in the car, never let the dog stick its head out of the window and cheerfully let its ears flap in the wind. The consequences for the dog could be serious inflammations of the ear and conjunctiva. If possible, during the hot season you should take your dog in the car only early in the morning and late in the evening.

If you walk your four-legged friend on hot days, make sure that you do not overtax the dog by taking a long walk. Particularly with older animals, on such days overexertion can easily lead to circulatory failure. Take your longer walks in the early morning and evening.

Exercise on hot days

During the "dog days" of summer, you must give the dog plenty of water, but — like humans — it needs less and lighter food. On hot days it is better to feed in several small portions. Also, avoid feeding during the afternoon heat. The dog prefers to eat in the morning or evening, when it is cool.

Provide proper nutrition

Even in hot weather, room temperature is ideal for dog food. Remove food stored in the refrigerator one hour before feeding.

When dogs cheerfully romp through a meadow in the summer, it often happens that blades of grass get stuck in the external ear. These enter the ear canal, and the more the animal tries to get rid of the foreign body by shaking its head vigorously, the deeper it penetrates. If the tip of the head is still visible, try to pull it out carefully. Usually, however, you will have to visit the veterinarian. Grass also gets stuck in the spaces between the foot pads. They can cause painful eczema and festering sores.

Grass

Fall

For large dogs that like to run, it is a pleasure to run alongside the owner's bi-

Cycling

cycle. To make sure that nothing happens, you must consider a few things:

- **Only well-trained dogs may go on bicycle rides**
  The dog must obey the owner to the letter! It should run to the right of the bicycle, so that it does not obstruct oncoming cyclists. It must stop immediately on command even without a leash, and in no case may it cross the street unless commanded to do so.
- **As a cyclist, you must adjust to the speed of the dog. Stop often at suitable places, and take a rest with your dog**.
- **Exercise brings on thirst**
  This also applies to dogs. Always bring a bottle of drinking water for your dog on bicycle rides, and do not forget the water dish.

Clipping and plucking

Make sure that your dog is plucked or clipped for the last time at the latest in October. If you do it later, the dog is in danger of catching cold.

Winter

Eating snow

Prevent your dog from doing this! Dogs like to eat large amounts of snow and pay for this with tonsillitis and gastroenteritis.

Tonsil–litis: Retching cough, vomiting

Gastroenteritis: The cold snow — in the city enriched with toxins, such as salt and other melting agents — harms the dog's intestinal flora. This leads to intense diarrhea and vomiting. The diarrhea may be watery and bloody. This condition is serious, because the dehydration and internal poisoning put an excessive strain on the circulation of the dog. The result can be circulatory failure. At the first symptoms of gastroenteritis, bring the dog to the veterinarian.

If it's eating snow, muzzle the dog before every walk. Before you put the muzzle on, sew a piece of linen into it to keep the snow from entering the openings. Gluing the muzzle shut with sticking plaster is not recommended, because it is impermeable to air.

Remedies for snow eating

When it snows or there is freezing rain, sand, salt, and other melting agents are spread on sidewalks and roads. The caustic chemicals not only melt the snow and ice, they also threaten the sensitive pads of the dog's paws. At first, the paws simply burn. Eventually they develop severe inflammations of the pads and the skin between the toes. In the advanced stage, the inflammation can become so painful that the dog can no longer walk. The dog needs veterinary treatment. Furthermore, the dog must be prevented from constantly licking and chewing at the inflamed paws. In the home, a light bandage or an old cotton sock usually offers adequate protection.

Inflamed, open paws

In the street the injured foot must be protected by a waterproof bandage. For this purpose you can also buy a plastic shoe and a sock with a non-slip plastic sole.

Dog shoes

Winter care
You can prevent injury to the paws through appropriate foot care before and after each walk. Before each walk, rub mink oil or a skin protectant containing silicone onto your dog's paws. Pet shops also offer special products for this purpose. By massaging these lightly onto the clean skin, a repellent protective film forms. After the walk, wash the paws with lukewarm water and dry them well with a soft, absorbent towel. Do not use soap or shampoo to wash the paws, because the skin, if it has already become irritated by salt and chemicals, could react by becoming inflamed.

Dog coats
Dogs with kidney or disc problems need a waterproof, warm coat in the cold and wet. There are plastic coats on the market that are lined with thick padding.

Dog grooming in the winter
Do not clip or pluck your dog in the winter. You should only bathe your four-legged friend in the winter if it is absolutely necessary (for example, medicinal baths).

DIET

The first commandment in dog nutrition is: the dog is no garbage disposal. Kitchen and table scraps are in no way suitable for the dog's diet. Only a properly fed dog can be a healthy dog.

The dog is what it eats

The carnivore misconception is widespread. Dogs that are fed exclusively with meat, however, get sick. We can trace this back to their wolf past. Wolves ate not only the muscle meat of the prey animals but also the stomach and intestines with the predigested vegetable matter they contained. In this way they also took up carbohydrates and fats. Wolves also ate bones, ligaments, tendons, and blood, and in this way met their mineral requirement.

Is the dog a pure carnivore?

Dogs that are fed meat exclusively soon become affected by meat-only syndrome. Although this diet supplies the dog with highly nutritious protein, the intake of minerals and vitamins is much too low. Deformities of the skeleton and painful joints appear. The dogs suffer from calcium deficiency. Moreover, they have poorly formed, foul-smelling stools. The coat becomes dull and the dogs lose weight. Due to the excess intake of protein, the liver and kidneys also become diseased.

The meat-only syndrome

Commercial food

You can nourish a dog optimally with commercial food alone, because it contains, besides meat, vegetable nutrients in a digestible form. Give precedence to wet food in cans. The canned food contains the basic nutrients: proteins, carbohydrates, and fats in the proper proportions. It also contains sufficient quantities of all the necessary vitamins and minerals. Exercise caution with dry food. You should avoid feeding dry food exclusively, because very few dogs will drink the extra amount of water they require to balance out the large amount of dry food. Calculi and stones in the urinary tract could be the result.

Does raw meat make dogs fierce?

Not feeding raw meat is a good practice. But there are important reasons why you should always cook the meat for your dog.

Dogs should not be fed raw meat, to rule out the danger of infection with salmonella, toxoplasmosis, and Pseudorabies.

Pseudorabies virus

This virus is often found in older pigs, without the animals themselves exhibiting symptoms. If dogs become infected by eating raw meat, they become restless, have a heavy flow of saliva, and intense itching. Pseudorabies is fatal to dogs. The disease is untreatable. So, do not neglect to cook the meat, because cooking kills the virus.

Entrails

Do not feed entrails and organs too often! If dogs eat large amounts, they can develop pathological symptoms. If, for example, you feed heart to your dog very frequently, eventual changes in the bones can occur. The calcium-phosphorus ratio is disturbed. Heart namely contains an excess of phosphorus. Liver, on the other hand, is extremely rich in vitamin A. It is so rich in this vitamin that vitamin A poisoning can result if liver is fed too frequently.

Salt

That dogs should eat no salt was formerly a widespread misconception. Today we know that every dog needs a small amount of salt. It is essential for the retention of water in the body. Commercial food already contains table salt in the required amount. Table salt is a particularly important component in the diet of dogs suffering from diarrhea, because it prevents the loss of excess water.

Fruit

Some dogs refuse to eat any fruit at all, while others even eat exotic fruits. If your dog shows an appetite for fruit, you should satisfy this need. Make sure, however, that the dog does not eat the pits—many pits are poisonous. Prune, apricot, and plum pits can also lead to intestinal obstruction, because they cling to the intestinal wall due to their rough surface. Furthermore, the pits contain small amounts of hydrocyanic acid, which can make, in particular, puppies sick.

Eggs

Cooked eggs are a source of easy-to-digest protein. Never feed them raw! Raw protein destroys the B vitamins and the biotin in the diet. Furthermore, cooking prevents an infection with salmonella.

Yeast   Yeast is completely harmless even in heavy doses. It is rich in B vitamins, and is particularly beneficial with older dogs. Yeast is also beneficial if the dog has liver damage.

Bones   Bones are not suitable as food! Apart from not having any nutritional value, they can be dangerous to the dog. The hydrochloric acid in the stomach is not present in sufficient quantity to dissolve an excess amount of bone. Undissolved pieces of bone harden the contents of the intestines and cause very unpleasant and dangerous bone-stool constipation. Poultry bones and the bones of wild game are particularly dangerous. They splinter easily and can penetrate the mucous membrane of the esophagus, stomach, or intestines, and even puncture the intestines. Pork chop or veal chop bones can easily get stuck in the throat or esophagus.

Why do dogs bury bones and leftover food?   We can trace this burying behavior back to the dog's wolf ancestry. In the wild you do not know what tomorrow will bring; wolves eat large quantities when they can. They bury and store the rest of the prey for hard times. Although our domestic dogs no longer have to capture their own food, they still retain much of these feeding instincts. They devour as much as they can and are extraordinarily fond of burying a supply of leftovers or bones in the yard, even though they know quite well that they are fed daily. Therefore, it is up to you to limit the amount of food.

Buried bones and leftovers become more digestible through aging, which corresponds to the ripening of cheese. In contrast to meat that spoils in the pot, meat that ages in the ground is not poisonous. The dog may therefore safely eat the meat. It is ripened in the same way as old cheese, and smells terrible to humans. The dog considers it to be a feast.

Are dug-up leftovers and bones spoiled?

You must never leave leftovers in the dish! As was mentioned above, food that spoils in the pot or the dish is poisonous to the dog. Leftovers in the dish can sour, become permeated with bacteria, or be colonized by fly maggots. The dog can get sick with severe food poisoning. If your dog regularly leaves part of the food in the dish, then simply reduce the dog's next ration. After the dog has finished eating, you must clean the dish thoroughly.

May you leave leftovers in the food dish?

Regardless of whether you prepare the food yourself or use commercial food, it must never be too cold or too hot. Never feed directly from the refrigerator, much less from the freezer! Always warm the food first. The microwave oven is very practical for this purpose. The ideal temperature for dog food is room temperature. In other words: serve the food lukewarm.

Temperature of the food

Water must be available to your four-legged friend around the clock. Always put its water dish in the same place, which must be easily accessible to the dog. Also, make sure that the dish is always filled with fresh water.

Drinking water

Milk

Whole milk is unsuitable as a drink for adult dogs. They cannot digest the lactose it contains, because they lack the necessary enzyme. The result of drinking milk is often diarrhea. Milk products such as cottage cheese or yogurt, however, can be valuable dietary supplements.

Does cheese destroy the sense of smell?

No, this is a superstition. Nevertheless, cheese does not necessarily belong in the food dish. Most kinds of cheese are too high in fat, and some are too highly seasoned.

Where should the food dish be?

The "table manners" of our four-legged friends vary greatly — some are decidedly clean eaters, others pull every piece of meat out of the dish before eating it. It is advisable to pick a place that is easy to clean. In most households the kitchen is well suited for this purpose. In the yard it must be a covered place. Always feed the dog in the same place. Naturally, the dog must have its peace and quiet when it eats.

How often should you feed a day?

Feed the adult dog once or twice a day. Always feed at the same time of day. If you feed only once a day, choose lunch time. In this way the dog will have enough time to relieve itself and will not have to go out at night. In any case, you must make sure that your dog can do its "business" five to six hours after eating.

Are treats allowed occasionally?

Do not get your dog used to treats at all. Otherwise, it will turn into a chronic beggar and become overweight, too. You should use treats only as a reward for good behavior, and as a teaching aid. Also, use only special dog snacks for this purpose. Sweets are strictly prohibited.

How much the four-legged friend should and may eat cannot be answered with precise amounts. You must determine for yourself the amount of food your dog needs to stay healthy and trim. As with humans, there are dogs with active and inactive metabolisms. A very active dog, of course, also needs more food than a lazy, inactive dog. To prevent obesity, you should weigh your four-legged friend regularly and keep a weight chart. If the dog has clearly gained weight, you must reduce the amount of food immediately.

How much may the dog eat?

With pedigreed dogs there is a prescribed ideal weight. It is best to ask about it when you buy the dog. Deviations above and below the ideal weight should not exceed ten percent. With mixed breeds, you must determine the ideal weight yourself by feeling the ribs and the backbone from time to time. With a dog of normal weight, you must be able to feel the ribs and backbone easily through the skin.

Is there an ideal weight for dogs?

Although a day of fasting a week is not an absolute "must" for a dog of normal weight, it is nevertheless recommended. A voluntary day of fasting cleanses the dog and corresponds to a human fast of only four hours.

Is a day of fasting a week beneficial?

Because of their wolf inheritance, many dogs want to eat as much as they can and

How can you tell if

101

Is the begging dog really hungry?

even beg for more food with a full stomach. If you are unsure whether your four-legged friend is really still hungry or the wolflike greed is coming through, then give it a slice of dry bread. If it eats the bread, it really is hungry.

Lack of appetite

First, have the veterinarian make sure the lack of appetite is not caused by an illness or a problem with the teeth. Then check to see if your male dog is "in love," or your female dog will soon go in heat. If none of this applies, then it is your job to stimulate your fellow-lodger's appetite. Often it is sufficient to put something particularly tasty — for example, some commercial cat food — on top of the food. Vitamin B supplements, such as brewer's yeast, stimulate the appetite. In particularly stubborn cases, have the veterinarian give the dog a few vitamin B injections.

Should the dog rest after eating?

Every dog needs to rest after eating. With large dogs, in particular, exercise immediately after eating can be life-threatening. With these dogs the full stomach could twist forward while jumping or running, which results in the dreaded bloat or acute gastric dilation-torsion.

Digestion

When you observe the digestion of your dog, you can tell if you are making mistakes in the diet.

Large quantities of stools show that you are feeding the dog low-quality food, which the body cannot utilize. Too much roughage (fiber) in the food also produces large quantities of stools. The less roughage in the food, the fewer stools are produced.

Few but black and smelly stools means that you are feeding too much meat.

When you feed your four-legged friend properly, its stools will be well formed, brown, and in an amount corresponding to the breed.

Severe flatulence

Foods high in fiber provide relief from flatulence. The high fiber content namely increases the amount of food that passes through the intestines, and thereby decreases the formation of gas and consequently the occurrence of flatulence. You can buy a fiber-rich diet from your veterinarian.

The most frequent result of poor nutrition is obesity.

Obesity

The causes of obesity are overfeeding, improper diet (too much fat and carbohydrate), too many "between-meal snacks," and too little exercise. Overweight dogs are prone to heart and circulatory disorders, diabetes, and damage to the locomatory apparatus, which simply cannot handle the excess weight.

How does obesity occur?

Commercial reduced-calorie dietetic food is available from your veterinarian. With it, the dog can lose weight without having to go hungry. The dietetic food can, of course, only work if it is fed exclusively. It is enriched with all essential vitamins and

Weight-loss diet with commercial dietetic food

minerals, so that the dog will not develop deficiency symptoms. The only other thing the obese four-legged friend gets is fresh drinking water.

What else can you do about obesity?

Make sure your dog gets plenty of exercise, because it supports the diet. Take frequent walks, and play with it more than normal. Also, give the four-legged friend plenty of attention, because love and affection can replace many "treats."

The weekly weight loss that you can expect with a dog amounts to — depending on the size of the dog — one to four pounds.

May an old dog be more obese?

The old dog should be even thinner than a young dog, because the energy requirement decreases by 20 percent in old age. This decrease in the caloric requirement begins at approximately eight years of age. Starting at this age, pay especially close attention to your pet's weight, and reduce the amount of food before it becomes overweight.

Diabetes

Diabetes occurs frequently in older, obese animals. Your veterinarian has special dietetic food for diabetic dogs. It is particularly high in fiber, and contains little fat and few carbohydrates. The high fiber content lowers the blood-sugar level after eating.

Food allergies

Dogs can suddenly react allergically to ingredients in food. These allergies can be expressed in three ways: as gastroenteritis with vomiting, diarrhea, or both; as itchy dermatitis; or as a combination of gastroenteritis and skin disorders.

Puppies need food that is richer in protein and minerals than do adult dogs. Well suited are the canned puppy foods, because their mineral content covers the higher requirements during the growth phase.

The nutrition of the puppy

Starting at about the third week of life, you should feed the puppies solid food to supplement the mother's milk.

Solid food

Suitable supplemental foods include canned puppy food and finely chopped cooked chicken. Moisten the food at first with oatmeal or rice gruel. As soon as the puppies start eating solid food, they also need drinking water.

Supplemental foods

Starting in the sixth week of life, you can switch the puppy to normal puppy food. Up to an age of three months, five meals a day are necessary. Subsequently, three feedings a day are sufficient, and starting in the seventh month you can acclimate the puppy to two meals a day.

When can the puppy get by without mother's milk?

You should feed puppy food preferably for the entire first year of life.

Puppy food

A rule of thumb is that puppies develop best when you feed them 80 percent of the amount of food that they would eat if unsupervised.

Growing dogs

If you try to accelerate growth by overfeeding with rich food, you can make serious

Large-dog growth

injuries, such as hip dysplasia, even worse. Essential for growing large dogs is, above all, that the calcium-phosphorus ratio is correct.

To achieve the ideal calcium-phosphorus ratio of 3:2, you can feed calcium supplements. With a dog weighing 20 pounds, it is sufficient to mix a tablespoon of whiting with the food daily. You can also use calcium-phosphorus preparations available from the veterinarian or the pharmacy.

Coping with an aggressive dog

If the dog is aggressive even toward its own family while eating, you can break it of the habit in the following way: Do not feed it in a corner, so that it does not feel under pressure, but tie it up. Do not offer it its food in its food dish, but rather in a large bowl. Then give it a small portion of the food in its dish. When it has eaten it, remove its food dish, go to the large bowl, fill the dish, and bring it back to the dog. Chat amiably with your four-legged friend all the while. If it now wags its tail amiably, it is time for the second step: Again, put a small portion of food in its dish. When it has finished eating, leave its dish where it is and fill it in place. Then leave it alone again. If this functions well, go to it while it is still eating, and toss a treat in the food dish. Give a treat that the dog is very fond of. Following this training, the dog will certainly no longer have anything against your being present while it eats.

Older dogs have a reduced metabolic rate with a lower energy requirement. Also, they can no longer digest protein as well. Therefore, feed old dogs only very nutritious, easily digestible protein, such as muscle meat and milk products. This eases the strain on the intestines and liver. Replace animal fats with vegetable fats, because they are easier for the dog to digest. Old dogs also need particularly large amounts of vitamins. You must feed supplements of vitamin A, B_1, B_2, B_6, B_{12}, and vitamin E. Vitamin E increases the resistance of older animals todisease.

Old dogs are susceptible to constipation because they no longer get as much exercise. To prevent constipation, feed a diet particularly high in fiber, which contains much roughage. You can either mix plenty of vegetables, fruit, and bran with the food, or buy a fiber-rich commercial food that was developed for this purpose.

Old dogs are prone to constipation

Serve your old four-legged friend several small meals, spread over the day. You should avoid large portions, because they could cause the diaphragm to be displaced forward and impair the function of the heart and lungs.

Feeding older dogs

HEALTH

First aid   *Bee and wasp stings*: Stings to the tongue or in the throat are dangerous because they can become very swollen. There is the danger of suffocation! Put ice cubes in the mouth, and bring the dog to the veterinarian as soon as possible!

Stings to the paws cause swelling and itching. A cold, wet compress or, better yet, a wrap with aluminum acetate provides relief.

Allergic   Some dogs react to insect stings by going
shock   into allergic shock. Circulatory collapse, shallow breathing, and general weakness are the result. The legs feel cold and the mucous membranes are pale or blue in color. Shock is always a life-threatening condition. Wrap the dog immediately in warm blankets, to keep it from losing too much heat, and take it to the veterinarian immediately!

Heat   The symptoms of heat stroke are rapid
stroke   panting, shivering, seizures, and loss of consciousness.

Bring the animal immediately into the shade or a cool room (basement!), spray it with cold water, and wrap the four-legged friend in cold, wet towels. Take the dog to the veterinarian without delay.

Profusely bleeding cuts

It is necessary to stop bleeding immediately; press a compress firmly on the bleeding wound. Do not clean the wound. Instead, take the dog to the veterinarian immediately. The veterinarian will dress the wound correctly and treat the loss of blood and circulatory shock.

Superficial abrasions

You may clean these yourself. First, remove the matted hair with blunt scissors, and then disinfect the wound. In the following days, bathe the wound several times a day with a medicinal application.

Bites

Dog bites often look harmless, but are always insidious! The canines of the rival dog tear deep "pockets" in the tissue under the skin. Because of the rapid growth of bacteria, abscesses often form. Therefore, clean bites thoroughly and have the veterinarian treat the dog with antibiotics within six hours.

Split or torn nails

Fill the crack with wax, so that it does not tear further. This will save the nail.

Seizures

Such attacks usually look more serious than they are. Place the animal gently on the ground, darken the room, and turn off all sources of noise, such as radios, televisions, and household appliances. Never try to administer medications or liquids to the animal during the attack. The seizures usually stop in a few minutes. Then place the four-legged friend on a blanket and bring it to the veterinarian. An accurate description of the attack will make the veterinarian's diagnosis and therapy easier.

Poisoning Symptoms include bleeding from the body cavities, vomiting, diarrhea, seizures, and loss of consciousness. As first aid, give the dog charcoal tablets to neutralize at least some of the poison. Then see the veterinarian as soon as possible!

Vomiting Do not feed the dog for a day. Give only mallow tea to drink. If the vomiting persists, you must take the dog to the veterinarian.

Diarrhea Withhold food for a day and offer only chamomile tea or weak black tea to drink. Because of the danger of dehydration, bring the dog to the veterinarian as soon as possible.

Bloat Large dogs, such as Great Danes and German Shepherds, or dogs with a broad thorax, such as Basset Hounds, are particularly susceptible to bloat, or acute gastric dilation-torsion. When bloating, the stomach swells up like a balloon and the dog collapses immediately. It is acutely life threatening! Only an immediate operation can save the dog.

Eye discharge Clean the eye with cotton wool soaked in chamomile tea and rub in the direction of the nose.

You may remove a foreign body from the eye if you can remove it easily. If this is not possible, place a wad of cotton wool soaked in cold chamomile on the eye, and bring the dog to the veterinarian immediately.

Foreign body in the eye

The dog constantly shakes its head and scratches at its ears. If head shaking suddenly appears and if the dog holds the head at an obvious tilt, there is probably a foreign body (for example, a head of grass) in the ear. If you can reach the foreign body, you may pull it out. If you cannot, you must consult the veterinarian. In any case, you may spray an ear-cleaning agent in the ear as first aid.

Ear ache

This kit (available from your veterinarian) contains all the necessary utensils, from medications to bandages to scissors, and so forth. It should provide stop-gap relief until you can consult the veterinarian.

"First aid kit"

Wet the coat of the affected part of the body with cold water. In this way you achieve the effect of a cold compress, which prevents further swelling and relieves the pain.

Sprains, bruises, and swelling

After a traffic accident, you must always suspect the presence of internal injuries! Until the animal ambulance shows up, lay the animal carefully on a blanket or piece of clothing and cover it. Caution: Injured animals could react defensively and bite out of fear or pain. Try to put on an improvised muzzle. Take a gauze bandage from the car's first-aid kit or a scarf, and

Traffic accidents

make a loose loop. Put this over the dog's muzzle and tighten it. First, knot the loop over the nose and then under the chin. Then run both ends around the neck and tie it behind the ears. Should the dog develop difficulty in breathing, you must untie the muzzle, open the mouth, and pull out the tongue.

When is a muzzle strictly forbidden?

When the dog has injuries to the thorax, or difficulty in breathing. With short-muzzled breeds (for example, Pekingese) you should not use a muzzle, because it could impair breathing.

How to remove paint, tar, and motor oil

Never try this with turpentine, gasoline, or other caustic chemicals. They could cause severe irritation of the skin. You can remove tar and grease effectively with vegetable oil. Then bathe the dog. The best way to remove paint is by carefully cutting out the matted hair.

Snake bite

Snake bites most often occur on the dog's head or paws. You will be able to see the two closely spaced punctures of the fangs. Important: calm the dog down, and immobilize it, because otherwise the toxin will spread through the body even faster. If the snake bite is on the paw, you should apply a pressure bandage above the bite, to keep the toxin from spreading as fast. Make sure that the bandage is not too tight, although the circulation must be reduced, it must not be cut off completely (danger of gangrene of the paw). Wrap the dog in a blanket and take it as quickly as possible to the veterinarian.

If these are only superficial, that is, the surface of the skin at the affected site is red and painful, but not broken, run cold water over it for a few minutes. Then apply a cold compress. If the burn or scald has also damaged deeper layers of skin, however, you may only cover the wound with a clean cloth then you must bring the dog immediately to the veterinarian.

Burns and scalds

This happens particularly with puppies that chew through electric cables. After an electric shock, dogs usually lie unconscious on their side, suffer burns, lose urine and feces, and sometimes also experience cardiac arrest. Never touch the animal as long as it is still in contact with the source of current. Turn off the current immediately! Then bring the dog to the veterinarian immediately.

Electric shock

Small, short-haired, young, and injured dogs are particularly susceptible to hypothermia. Animals suffering from hypothermia feel cold, shiver, have strongly dilated pupils, and a below-normal body temperature (below 38° C). Warm the dog slowly by wrapping it in a warm blanket. Place a hot-water bottle on the outside of the blanket — not directly on its coat! Dogs suffering from hypothermia may burn easily, because the skin has very poor circulation. Finally, you can give the dog a warm bath. The water temperature should be 39 to 40° C. Make sure that its head stays above water.

Hypothermia

Drowning   This happens above all following a fall into a swimming pool, because dogs cannot climb the ladder to get out. After rescuing the four-legged friend from the water, pull its tongue out, and make sure that the water can run out by letting the dog hang its head down. You can lift small dogs by the hind legs and swing them slowly back and forth, until no more water flows out. You must never pick up large dogs by the hind legs, because you could injure the hips. Hold large dogs tightly by the belly while letting them hang head down. Carefully compress the thorax repeatedly until no more water comes out. In the following days, the dog should be kept under veterinary supervision.

Preventive medicine   *Taking the temperature*: Lubricate the thermometer, clamp the dog between your legs, and lift the tail with one hand. With the other hand insert the thermometer deep into the anus, if possible up to the 40° C (104° F) graduation line. Under no circumstances let go of the thermometer as long as it is inserted in the dog's anus. It is best to tie a string tightly around the indented end of the thermometer, so that you can pull it out quickly should the dog get restless. Depending on the dog's size and age, the normal temperature is 38 to 38.5° C (100.4° F). Small breeds and puppies have a higher temperature than large breeds and old animals. Never take the temperature immediately following a meal or after physical exertion, because the temperature rises slightly at these times.

Because many laypersons have a hard time taking their dog's pulse by pressing on the large femoral artery on the inside of the thigh, you can count the heartbeats instead. For this purpose, place one hand on the dog's chest directly below the left elbow joint. Move your hand around until you feel the heartbeat. Then count the number of beats in 20 seconds and multiply the result by three. An example: You have counted 35 beats in the 20 seconds. This means that the dog in question has a pulse rate of 105 beats per minute. With large breeds, the normal pulse rate is 80 to 100 beats per minute, with small breeds, 100 to 120.

Taking the pulse

A healthy dog takes 10 to 40 breaths per minute. Watch the thorax and count how often it rises in 20 seconds. Multiply the result by three. It would be wrong to count both the rise and fall of the thorax.

Number of breaths per minute

Most veterinary clinics are equipped with an animal scale, so you should make sure on each visit to the veterinarian that your dog is weighed and the result recorded. If you want to weigh your dog at home, you must pick up the dog and weigh yourself with the animal. Then put the dog down and weigh yourself alone. You calculate the dog's weight by subtracting your weight from the combined weight. Ask your veterinarian about your dog's ideal weight.

Weighing

Combination vaccinations: When the puppy is about 12 weeks old, you can start with the combination, active immu-

Vacci‐ nations

nizations. They protect the dog against distemper, infectious canine hepatitis, leptospirosis, canine parvovirus, and rabies. In the first year all vaccinations must be repeated after three weeks. In subsequent years, an annual booster shot is required. Only then is your dog safely protected.

Preventive deworming

Even if the dog shows no symptoms of a worm infestation, you should have it dewormed at least twice a year with a broad-spectrum deworming agent.

Therapeutic deworming is always indicated when you notice "worm symptoms."

Tapeworms

Near the place where the dog sleeps, you notice objects resembling grains of rice. These are the dried-out segments of tapeworms. Because the tapeworm segments pass actively out of the anus, they cause itching, and the dog exhibits the typical sliding on the hindquarters. The veterinarian can bring quick relief with a special tapeworm medication.

Roundworms

Noodle-like white structures appear in the dog's stool. A heavy roundworm infestation also causes anemia, diarrhea, and vomiting. The veterinarian prescribes a special roundworm medication.

Fleas

Fleas are extremely detrimental to the health. They are the intermediate hosts for tapeworms and are responsible for anemia, itching, and allergy to fleas.

Stand the dog on a white surface, and comb it against the grain of the hair. Any black dots that appear on the substrate are flea feces. To be absolutely sure, sprinkle a little water on the dots. If they turn red, this indicates the presence of undigested blood in the flea feces.

Recog-nizing a flea infest-ation

To prevent a flea infestation, the dog should always wear a flea collar, which you must replace regularly. If your dog has very sensitive skin, simply place the flea collar over the normal collar.

Flea pre-vention

Ticks transmit borreliosis, and in warmer regions also babesiosis.

Ticks

You can now buy protective collars that prevent a tick infestation, and they are used in conjunction with a flea collar.

Tick preven-tion

These scent glands alongside the anus must be drained from time to time to prevent the fluid inside from becoming impacted and inflamed.

Emptying the anal sacs

Dogs also need an annual veterinary checkup. The checkup consists of blood and urine tests, x-rays of the heart and lungs, and a thorough clinical examination of the four-legged friend by the veterinarian.

Checkup at the veterin-arian

To keep the gums and teeth healthy, the veterinarian must remove tartar at least once a year with ultrasound.

Tartar

Ten tips for how you can keep your dog healthy:

Tips

1. If you have a pedigreed dog, find out what diseases the breed is susceptible to. Have the veterinarian examine the dog regularly for these ailments.
2. Make sure the puppy receives vaccinations against infectious diseases and is dewormed in a timely manner. Do not forget the annual booster shots.
3. It is best to combine the annual booster shots with a preventive veterinary checkup.
4. Do not try to accelerate the growth of your dog through overfeeding and too rich a diet. This could cause permanent damage to the skeleton.
5. In the course of daily care, check the skin, eyes, and ears, so that you can spot pathological changes in time.
6. In any case, avoid overfeeding the dog.
7. Keep your dog's sleeping place, and the food and water dishes meticulously clean. Scrupulous hygiene is an important factor in maintaining your dog's health.
8. Keep the dog itself very clean, and watch out for discharges in the anal and genital region.
9. Never leave your dog unsupervised outside your own property! Stray dogs often cause traffic accidents or become involved in fights with other dogs. Both can lead to serious injuries or even death.
10. Take your dog for a walk every day — even if you have a large yard. The walk not only keeps the dog and you slim and healthy, it also gives you the opportunity to review its lessons and commands.

THE DOG AND THE VETERINARIAN

Ideally, a single veterinarian is sufficient to care for your dog throughout its life. In fact, the better the veterinarian knows your dog, the more quickly he will notice changes from the normal state of health. The veterinarian will also recognize possible character traits of your pet and can take them into account in his dealings with the dog. Furthermore, the veterinarian's records contain all the important information about your dog, such as vaccinations, dewormings, illnesses, laboratory results, and medications.

How many veterinarians should the dog have?

If possible, choose a veterinarian near your home to spare the dog from a long drive when it is sick. Make sure that the veterinarian is sympathetic to you and instills confidence in you. Watch to see if he handles his four-legged patients lovingly and patiently. The dog notices, just as the human does, if it is being treated as an "important personality" or merely as "one patient among many."

Choosing the veterinarian

THE DOG AND THE VETERINARIAN

The first visit to the veterinarian

Regardless of whether you have acquired a puppy or an adult dog, take it as soon as possible to the veterinarian you trust. In this way, a timely plan for vaccinations and deworming can be worked out, and the dog and veterinarian can become acquainted in an undramatic situation.

How often should the dog see the veterinarian?

You should visit the veterinarian with your dog at least once a year, both for the purpose of the preventive veterinary checkup and for the annual vaccinations. Old dogs must visit the veterinarian twice a year.

House calls

Request a house call only if you have absolutely no other choice. First, a house call if available at all is considerably more expensive than the same treatment at the office, and, second, dogs are usually far more disciplined at the veterinary clinic than in the security of their familiar surroundings. Furthermore, the lighting conditions in private homes are usually inadequate for a thorough examination. At the veterinary clinic, the veterinarian also has access to trained personnel and all the necessary technical examination equipment. The equiment makes it easier to diagnose the patient.

The trip to the veterinarian

Because most dogs like to ride in the car and are also used to it, the trip to the veterinarian is rarely a problem.

Always bring the dog's vaccination certificate! If the dog is taking medications, show them to the veterinarian. If you have noticed anything unusual in the dog's stool or vomit, bring a specimen of it.

Describe precisely to the veterinarian anything out of the ordinary you may have noticed with your dog recently. Information about changes in behavior is often just as important as the stool sample for the diagnosis. You should be able to answer the following questions: Does the dog eat? How much does it drink? Can it defecate and urinate, and when was the last time it relieved itself? What is the appearance of the stool and urine? Have you noticed blood in the urine or stool? Does the dog vomit? What does the vomit look like, and at what intervals does it vomit? Does the dog cough, and how does the cough sound? Does the dog have difficulty in standing up or moving? Does it show pain?

What will the veterinarian want to know?

While training your dog, also consider the handling your four-legged friend will have to put up with during the veterinary examination. Accustom your dog to handling early on. It should not be a problem to push up the dog's flews and to open the mouth. A well-trained dog willingly allows the veterinarian to put it on the examination table, to lift its paws individually, and to look in its ears.

What the dog will have to put up with

Simple indigestion: The dog vomits, but has a normal stool. The reason for this is usually a single improper feeding. Also, the dog may have eaten something it should not have on its walk. To cure simple indigestion, in most cases, a day of fasting and

Is my dog sick?

administering chamomile or mallow tea is sufficient.

What is the significance of vomiting?

Gastritis: If the vomiting lasts longer than one day with a normal stool, you must suspect an inflammation of the stomach lining, that is, gastritis. To cure gastritis, a veterinary treatment and a special diet are necessary.

Volvulus: If the dog vomits constantly and is unable to pass its stool at the normal time, volvulus must be suspected. This is life threatening and requires an operation.

Uremia: With uremia, toxic substances enter the bloodstream because of kidney disease. Characteristic of uremic dogs is that they exhibit excessive thirst, but very quickly vomit up the liquid again. In the final stages, the symptoms include diarrhea, seizures, and the vomiting of blood.

What is the significance of excessive thirst?

Diabetes: This is the abbreviated form of the term "diabetes mellitus." The excessive thirst that is a symptom of this disease is caused by the increased urine volume because of the excretion of sugar. The veterinarian can easily determine if diabetes mellitus is actually present by means of a test. Treatment involves a special diet and insulin injections.

Diabetes insipidus: This disease is triggered by the reduced function of the pituitary gland. With this disease the dog excretes a great deal of urine and has a correspondingly great thirst. Urine amounts of five liters with a medium-sized dog are possible with this disease. The veterinarian makes the diagnosis by means of a laboratory test. Diabetes insipidus is treated with injections.

Pyometra: This is the term for a uterine infection in which the uterus fills with pus. The symptoms, besides excessive thirst, include apathy, loss of appetite, vomiting, and a dull coat. In most cases the uterus must be removed.

Fever: If the body temperature is elevated, the dog drinks more.

The dog — like the human being — has a cough center in the brain. This center can be stimulated by various factors.

Foreign body: When small foreign bodies, such as small wood splinters, get stuck in the throat, the windpipe, or the bronchia, the result is an intense dry cough. If the dog is unable to cough up the foreign body, the veterinarian must remove it. Some foreign bodies — particularly those in the bronchia — can only be detected by means of an x-ray.

Tonsillitis: Retching cough and the vomiting of white foam always indicate tonsillitis. In the dog, the tonsils normally are retracted in pouches in the mucous membrane.

In the case of severe tonsillitis, however, the tonsils become swollen and protrude from the pouches in the mucous membrane. The dog now thinks it has foreign bodies in its throat, and tries to bring them up by gagging and coughing. You absolutely must visit the veterinarian, because chronic tonsillitis has a negative effect on the heart and joints.

Acute laryngitis: Symptoms of acute laryngitis include painful bouts of coughing.

Worm bronchitis: This occurs primarily in very young dogs. It is caused by roundworm larvae. The larvae also infest the bronchia as they wander through the body.

Congestive bronchitis: Old dogs are particularly susceptible to this ailment. Because of the aging heart, the circulation is impaired, and fluids are retained in the bronchia.

Infectious bronchitis: It occurs as an accompanying symptom of infectious diseases.

The significance of drooling? A foreign body in the mouth produces a heavy flow of saliva. Bones and pieces of wood often wedge themselves between the molars of the upper jaw. Besides the flow of saliva, you will notice that the dog raises its paw to its mouth repeatedly. Reach inside the mouth, and remove the foreign body.

Tartar, gingivitis, and tumors of the gums can also cause excessive drooling.

They occur with the heavy infestation of roundworms in puppies.

Tapeworm infestation: The tapeworm segments that actively pass out of the anus cause itching, and the dog exhibits the typical sliding on the hindquarters.

Impacted or inflamed anal sacs produce a feeling of pressure, itching, and pain. To counteract these symptoms, the dog slides across the ground on its hindquarters.

This is a clear symptom of the open form of the infection of the uterus (pyometra). The female dog requires an operation.

Flatulence, combined with light-colored, sticky diarrhea: These symptoms indicate a chronic disease of the pancreas or liver.

Bright-red urine: In this case, the entire urine is mixed with blood, thus producing the color. The reason for this is kidney disease or poisoning.

Dripping blood following urination: This is a symptom of an inflammation of the bladder or the urethra. Make sure that the dog drinks plenty of fluids, and take the dog to the veterinarian.

If the urine is released only in a trickle, this is a symptom of an obstruction of the urethra by bladder stones or urinary calculus. Because a life-threatening uremia

"Hiccups"

Brownish vaginal discharge

Flatulence

Blood in the urine?

Trickling urination

can result from the backing up of the urine, the veterinarian must remove the stones or calculus immediately.

Sudden accidents

When dogs that were previously "housebroken" suddenly relieve themselves inside the house again, the reason usually is not a physical ailment, but rather a psychological disorder. Consider if there have been changes in the daily routine and in the environment of the dog.

Ear problem

If the dog frequently scratches at its ears and frequently shakes its head vigorously, it probably is suffering from an infection of the ear canal. If the ear canal is also filled with a brownish-black discharge, the dog is infested with ear mites.

Head tilt

Head tilt can be an indication of a foreign body or a tumor in the ear.

When the ear flap suddenly swells

Because of vigorous head shaking with an ear infection, a hematoma develops between the cartilage and skin of the year. The ear flap appears as if it is inflated. The veterinarian must operate to remove the blood clot.

Itching

Itching is always a symptom of a skin disease.

Itching and circular, hairless patches of skin indicate ringworm.

Itching in association with severe hair loss and scaly lesions indicates the presence of mange mites.

Severe itching over the entire body is often triggered by fleas, and an allergy to fleas.

This can be caused by an inflammation of the conjunctiva, but can also be the first symptom of distemper. Only the veterinarian can diagnose what it really is. Generally, it is true that a clear, transparent eye discharge is not dangerous and you can plan the visit to the veterinarian to fit into your schedule. A thick, pus-like discharge, however, is a sign of a serious infection. You should go to the veterinarian immediately.

Eye discharge

All dogs have, on the inside of the third eyelid, a tear gland — the so-called nicitating membrane gland — which you normally, do not see. Occasionally, it swells and becomes visible as a small sphere under the third eyelid. It looks as if the dog has a little cherry in the eye. The veterinarian must operate to remove the enlarged nicitating membrane gland.

Small red sphere in the inner corner of the eye

Drops of pus at the tip of the penis indicate an infection of the prepuce. This disease can be transmitted to other dogs and, therefore, is very widespread. Have the veterinarian prescribe an appropriate medication for local treatment.

Pus at the tip of the penis

If the dog repeatedly tries unsuccessfully to defecate, something is wrong. It is possible that a foreign body is stuck in the intestines or the animal has impacted feces.

Constipation

Yellowish discoloration of the skin, conjunctiva, and gums

This is a serious alarm signal! It usually indicates jaundice as a consequence of a serious liver disease or a disorder of the blood. The animal requires immediate veterinary treatment.

Here, too, you must visit the veterinarian as soon as possible. Extreme paleness can be a symptom of anemia, as well as life-threatening internal bleeding.

Dark coloration of the skin

As a consequence of chronic skin irritation, dark-colored even black patches often result. This is the case, for example, when the dog constantly gnaws on an area that itches. It is, so to speak, a self protection by the skin — it thickens and darkens.

Hairless calluses on the elbow and knee

These thickened areas of skin are caused by lying on hard surfaces. They are particularly common in large, heavy dogs. If nothing is done about them, these calluses can cause problems. The best preventive measure against calluses is a soft mattress to lie on.

Lumps and tumors under the skin

Individual lumps and tumors of the skin are no reason for panic, because very often they are simply benign enlargements of the sebaceous glands or warts that require no treatment. Nevertheless, you should visit the veterinarian if you find a lump, because only he can determine whether or not a closer examination of the new growths is necessary. Particularly with older dogs, you must consider that the tumors could be malignant.

If the four-legged friend suddenly develops a hemispherical, hot swelling, which is tough and hard at first, but becomes soft and elastic after a few days, it is probably an abscess. This is a collection of pus under the skin. The cause is usually a very small puncture wound, such as a bite suffered in a fight. An abscess must be drained by the veterinarian.

Hot spot

This condition occurs predominantly in short-muzzled breeds, such as the Pekingese. These animals do not breathe through the nose, but rather snore through the mouth. During physical exertion or excitement, the snoring breathing sounds intensify. The reason for this is usually an excessively long soft palate, which, however, can be surgically shortened.

Snoring breathing sounds

Limping in a dog can have a number of causes: fractures, sprains, ligament damage, or congenital defects. Often, however, slight limping can be traced back simply to overexertion. In this case even an aspirin provides relief. To determine the cause, in any case, you should take the dog to the veterinarian.

Limping

Dogs roll enthusiastically in stinking, repulsive things. This is not pathological, however, but rather has its roots in the dog's wolf past. The stench masked the wolves' own scent, and the prey they were stalking did not suspect that they were

"Perfuming" with carrion and worse

nearby. It is nearly impossible to break a dog of this predilection.

Alarm signals with puppies

With puppies, in particular, you must be prepared to visit the veterinarian at the slightest symptom of illness, because the little organism can become unbalanced in a very short time. You must watch for the following alarm signals: A sudden change in temperament can indicate a problem. Apathy, the refusal of food and water, limping for no apparent reason and constantly whimpering quietly to itself, thick discharge from the eyes and nostrils, smelly ears, vomiting, and diarrhea are all indications that you must bring the puppy to the veterinarian as soon as possible. Do not waste valuable time through senseless delay.

Is it good to be unusually attentive in case of sickness?

It is completely natural for you to want to give your sick pet an unusual amount of love and attention when it is sick. Although a certain amount of it is also necessary, you should never totally spoil the dog. After all, the four-legged friend does not understand why it is being showered with so much extra affection and why it is suddenly allowed to do things that it previously was forbidden. When it is healthy again, it will not understand why the extreme attention is over and that it should behave normally again. This turns it into an insecure, anxious, and maybe also a tiresome dog.

Treat the sick dog considerately, but do not worship it. Do not hold it constantly in your lap, and do not spoil it with treats — except when you are using them to administer medications. Give the patient only as much consideration as the illness warrants. In general, treat the dog as you normally do. In this way you will prevent your pet from retaining emotional damage after it regains its physical health.

When the dog needs medication
Administering tablets

Hide tablets, that do not have too strong an odor, inside a treat. If you tease the dog a little with it, it will finally snatch the treat and swallow it immediately without a second thought. This method does not work with tablets that have a very strong odor (such as penicillin). You must insert these tablets with your fingers well back on the tongue in the throat. Then pull your hand out quickly and hold the muzzle shut until the dog has swallowed the tablet. You can trigger the swallowing reflex by massaging the throat.

Liquid medication

Never simply pour liquids into the gaping mouth, because in this way the dog could spit out most of the medication. The right way to do it is to hold the dog's muzzle (with nose pointing up), while a second person pulls the corner of the lips away from the teeth and pours in the medication. To encourage swallowing, you can again massage the throat.

Giving eyedrops

First, you must clean the eye with a wad of cotton wool soaked in chamomile tea. Important: Always clean from the outside corner of the eye in toward the nose! Then reach around the dog's eye with your index finger on the upper lid and the thumb on the lower lid. Pull the lower lid down with your thumb and drip the liquid into the pocket you have created.

Applying eye ointment

First, clean the eye as above and reach around the eye with the thumb and index finger. Then pull the lower lid down again with your thumb, and, depending on the size of the dog, squeeze a 1 to 2 centimeter long bead of ointment into the lid pocket. Now draw the upper and lower lid over the bead of ointment to carefully distribute the ointment in the eye.

Ear drops

Hold the tip of the dog's ear and lift it up to expose the ear canal. Then insert the tip of the plastic ear-drop bottle as deeply into the ear canal as possible and give the bottle a good squeeze. It is impossible to count the number of ear drops; it is also unnecessary. Better a little too much than too little. Finally, massage the cartilage below the ear opening up and down. This produces a sloshing sound, which indicates that the ear drops are being distributed throughout the ear canal.

Rubbing with liquids

Always rub in liquids against the grain of the hair, because this is the only way to reach the skin, where, of course, the liquids are supposed to take effect. With very long-haired dogs, you must part the hair repeatedly to get the liquid to the skin.

Applying ointments

Always apply ointments immediately before walking the dog. The abundance of smells on the walk will distract the dog, so that it does not lick off the ointment. The ointment can do its work in peace.

In principle, all animals — including the dog — can be infected with toxoplasmosis, but not all animals can transmit it. The pathogen is a sporozoan *(Toxoplasma gondii)*, which during pregnancy can injure or kill the human fetus. Important for the dog owner: Dogs are not carriers! They do not shed any infectious toxoplasmids. Therefore, it is impossible to be infected with toxoplasmosis by your dog.

Danger of infection by the dog Toxoplasmosis

Rabies is caused by a virus that causes severe inflammation of the central nervous system and ultimately leads to death. The principal carrier and principal vector of the virus is the red fox. The percentage of rabid dogs, fortunately, is very low. The disease is transmitted by contact with the saliva of rabid animals when they bite. The rabies virus cannot penetrate unbroken skin. Bites through clothing are less serious, because the textile fibers have a certain filtering effect. The symptoms of rabies in the dog have, however, changed. The formerly known "furious stage" is often absent today. "Paralytic rabies" usually predominates. The symptoms of paralytic rabies are vague; only a veterinarian can make the proper diagnosis.

Rabies

Because rabies is also life-threatening for humans, you absolutely must have your dog vaccinated against rabies. The basic immunization consists of two vaccinations

Rabies prevention

given at an interval of three weeks. An annual booster shot is necessary.

Because the vaccinated dog itself cannot contract rabies, it also cannot transmit rabies.

Biting Never run away to avoid trouble. If your dog has been vaccinated properly against rabies, show the vaccination certificate to the injured person and the attending doctors. This calms down the person who was bitten, and in many cases spares him or her from the postexpositional rabies vaccination.

An unvaccinated dog has bitten If a human being has been bitten, it is important to wash out the wound immediately with plenty of soap and water, and to treat it with a disinfectant (70-percent alcohol, tincture of iodine). Then the person must go to the doctor immediately. The dog's owner must take his dog twice to the veterinarian for the prescribed rabies examination. The first examination should, if possible, take place on the day of the bite. The second examination is performed 10 days after the bite.

A strange dog has bitten If the "biter" was able to get away without having been identified beforehand, the bitten person must begin the postexpositional rabies vaccination immediately. This is the vaccination that is administered to people following injury by a rabid animal or one that is suspected of being rabid. This protective measure must take place as soon as possible. The first vaccination following a bite consists of two injections, one in the left and one in right upper arm. The second series of injections takes place two weeks later, and the third two weeks after that. With very serious bites, the doctor additionally sprays the wound with immune serum (complete antibodies).

Preventive rabies vaccination is generally recommended only for occupational groups that are at risk, such as veterinarians, animal keepers, farmers, butchers, and so forth. Naturally, anyone who feels in danger can get protection. The basic immunization consists of two vaccinations, with the second given 28 days after the first. The first booster shot is administered six to 12 months later. Additional booster shots are required every five years.

Preventive vaccination against rabies for humans

The rabies vaccination is completely harmless, because the rabies vaccine is a so called "killed vaccine". This means that it contains only killed viruses, which cannot produce any symptoms of the disease.

Is the rabies vaccination dangerous for humans?

This disease is caused by spirochete bacteria. Sources of infection for dogs are conspecifics, but rats and mice can be carriers, too. Usually, however, dogs become infected through contact with the urine of infected conspecifics, sometimes also while bathing in standing bodies of water. Leptospirosis is communicable to humans! The principal source of infection for humans is the urine of infected dogs. The clinical picture with humans is similar to

Leptospirosis

that of dogs. Fever, jaundice, nephritis, vomiting, and diarrhea are the most important symptoms.

How can humans protect themselves against leptospirosis?

The most important and simplest measure is the regular vaccination of your dog against leptospirosis. When handling a dog infected with leptospirosis, the most meticulous cleanliness is indicated. If you must handle the urine of the infected dog (for example, to collect a urine sample or to wipe up a puddle of urine from the floor), always wear disposable gloves. If you have minor wounds on the hands, you must be particularly careful, because they are ideal points of entry for the leptospirosis bacteria.

Tuberculosis

This disease rarely occurs in dogs. The owner of a tubercular dog will notice a cough that is resistant to therapy, emaciation, digestive disorders, and elevated temperature. If a dog is diagnosed with tuberculosis, the whole family must be tested immediately for the disease. Tuberculosis is treatable, but the therapy extends over a fairly long period of time — at least six months.

Scabies

This condition is caused by microscopically small parasites: scabies mites. The dog suffers from intense itching, severe hair loss, and the formation of pustules, nodules, and scabs.

Sometimes humans who have close contact with dogs infected with scabies develop itchy nodules on the torso and arms. We should not confuse these skin manifestations, however, with true human scabies, because the scabies mites of the dog cannot survive and reproduce on humans. The nodules they produce disappear on their own in three to four weeks, whereas human scabies requires more intensive therapy.

Unfortunately, ringworm occurs relatively frequently in dogs. Because the ringworm fungus can be transmitted from dogs to humans, it is particularly important to recognize ringworm on your four-legged friend as soon as possible. In the dog, ringworm occurs most frequently on the head and legs. Circular, hairless lesions, broken hairs, as well as scaling and reddening of the skin are alarm signals that require an immediate trip to the veterinarian. With severely infected dogs, the hair becomes covered with such heavy encrustations that you can even see them with the naked eye. Itching can occur, but is not always present. If the veterinarian has made the diagnosis of "ringworm," you must thoroughly disinfect the dog's environment. The reason for this is that humans can be infected not just through the direct contact with the dog, but rather also through objects such as brushes, combs, blankets, upholstery, dandruff, hair, and so forth. It is essential to keep the dog's environment as clean as possible, because ringworm spores can remain viable for years in a dry environment.

Ringworm

Because dogs frequently have worms, many dog owners are afraid of being infected with

Worms

worms by their dog. Therefore, it is important to have the veterinarian explain how to control worms on the first visit. Furthermore, at the slightest suspicion of a worm infestation, you should visit the veterinarian immediately, to prevent the propagation of the parasites through timely treatment. It is possible today to successfully control all the kinds of worms affecting dogs simultaneously with a single broad-spectrum deworming agent. The deworming of the puppy, and subsequently the regular preventive deworming of the dog, is a matter of course.

Round-worms

If your dog has roundworms, you will notice fairly long, whitish structures in the feces. These are the sexually mature roundworms. The consequences of a roundworm infestation are diarrhea, anemia, and developmental disorders. Puppies that are already born with roundworms exhibit the typical distended "puppy belly," cough, and poor overall condition. Roundworms lay their eggs in the dog's intestines. These pass out of the body with the feces, where they are ingested by another dog. Then they again develop into sexually mature roundworms in the intestines of the other dog.

Can the dog infect humans with round-worms?

In principle, humans can get infected while playing with infected dogs, because the roundworm eggs cling to the dog's coat and stick to the hands while petting. If the human then sucks on the fingers, he or she becomes infected. Infection is also possible through dog feces — for example, in the sandbox.

Are round-worms dangerous for humans?

They are not dangerous, because the round-worm eggs that are ingested by humans cannot develop normally, because humans are an unsuitable host. After moving around in the body for a short time, the worm larvae encapsulate themselves in organs or muscles. Usually no significant symptoms of illness appear, because the human immune system defends itself successfully. In exceptional cases there can be a slight fever, which rarely impairs vision.

Preventing infection

Besides the regular deworming of the puppy, following strict hygienic guidelines is helpful: Keep your puppy's bed clean, and bathe the dog to remove any round-worm eggs that may be clinging to the coat. Do not let the dog lick your face and hands. In consideration of other people, you should make sure that your dog does not defecate in playgrounds, much less in sandboxes.

Tape-worms

All tapeworms have in common that they need an intermediate host, which is then eaten by the final host — thus, the dog. The kind of tapeworm species that will infect our four-legged friend therefore depends on which intermediate host it has access to.

Pumpkin-seed-like tape-worms

This is the most common tapeworm in the dog. It requires the flea as the intermediate host for its development. The pumpkin-seed-shaped tapeworm segments which the eggs pass out of the dog's body with the feces. These cling to the dog's coat and are ingested by canine fleas. If the flea now bites the dog, it becomes infected with the tapeworm. A heavy infestation leads to stomach ache, diarrhea, emaciation, and anemia. When humans are infected with the pumpkinseed-like tapeworm, symptoms similar to those of the dog are exhibited. This is unpleasant, but not dangerous.

The three-segmented tapeworm

This is one of the dangerous *Echinokokken* species. For its development, the canine three-segmented tapeworm needs the horse, cow, sheep, goat, or pig as its intermediate host. The virulent worms develop in the liver and lung of the intermediate host. If the intermediate host is butchered and the worm-infested liver and lung are fed to the dog, the dog will be infected with the three-segmented tapeworm.

Which dogs are in danger?

Rural dogs are at high risk, because they are often fed uninspected entrails from home-slaughtered livestock. City dogs are at lower risk.

Is the three-segmented tapeworm dangerous for humans?

Yes, even life-threatening! Humans, too, can serve as the intermediate host. This means that the tumorlike, proliferating cysts also develop in humans. They grow like a tumor in the liver and lung and can reach the size of a child's head. They cause serious symptoms of illness and occasionally lead to death.

The human being becomes infected through intensive contact with infected dogs, because *Echinokokkus* eggs stick to the coat and from there can reach the human mouth.

SEXUALITY

Female dogs become sexually mature — depending on the breed — at 6 to 12 months. Estrus first occurs at this age. Small breeds go in heat earlier than large breeds.

Sexual maturity

Male dogs are sexually mature and thus capable of breeding at 8 to 12 months of age.

Most bitches go in heat twice a year. There are, however, exceptions. Some go in heat only once a year, while others surprise their owners with three heats a year.

How often does the bitch go in heat?

The heat lasts about three weeks.

Duration

Bitches that have not been sterilized go in heat even in old age, and can still have puppies.

Proestrus: The vulva enlarges and swells. The dog's owner will notice a bloody discharge.

Phases of the heat

Estrus: In this phase — it lasts from the 9th to the 16th day — the bitch tolerates coitus. This is the so-called "standing time." The discharge diminishes and becomes paler in color.

Diestrus: This phase is outwardly noticeable for about a week. The vulva returns to normal and at most remnants of a discharge are still present.

Dog "panties"

These are offered on the market, and protect floors, carpets, and upholstery during estrus.

Removing traces of blood

You can remove traces of blood dripped by bitches in heat from carpet with glass cleaner. Spray the stain thoroughly, and wipe it up with a damp, hot cloth.

Keeping "amorous" male dogs away

Chlorophyll pills (dog-stop pills) neutralize the scent of the bitch in heat and keep the "love-crazed" male dog in check. Administer the pills from the beginning and throughout the period of estrus.

When "love" triumphs

Despite all precautions of the dog owner, it still sometimes happens that the male dog finds its way to its "beloved." Nevertheless, in no case give in to your first impulse to pull the two dogs apart or to pour cold water over the two of them. For as soon as the male dog inserts its penis, the glans penis becomes very swollen. For this reason, the animals still remain coupled together in the mating position for 10 to 30 minutes following ejaculation. A forceful separation would cause injury to the vagina and glans penis.

Approximately six to eight weeks after estrus, some bitches become restless and begin to mother certain objects.

False pregnancy

Purely externally you will notice strongly swollen teats in the bitch. Often milk even drips from them. In the initial stage, you can put compresses of aluminum acetate (or mixtures of therapeutic earth and vinegar water) on the inflamed teats. Treatment with heparin ointments have also proved effective. You can also moisten the teats several times a day with cold water. This, too, will reduce the swelling and milk production.

Never squeeze out the milk, because this would only serve to stimulate milk production.

The less the bitch eats and drinks, the sooner milk production will subside.

The more you distract the bitch from the imagined motherhood, the shorter the duration of the false pregnancy. Take extended walks and play lovingly with the animal. You should not promote the maternal instinct of the bitch, and it is therefore advisable to take away toys such as rubber dolls, cushions, and anything the bitch could use to build a nest.

Psychological care during false pregnancy

If you are certain that your bitch should never have puppies, you should have it

Spaying the bitch

spayed. Spaying is the removal of the ovaries and uterus. Following spaying, the bitch changes neither its character, nor will it get obese as long as you do not overfeed it.

Benefits of spaying

The spayed bitch no longer goes in heat and can no longer develop a false pregnancy. Furthermore, spaying is the best way to prevent tumors of the mammary glands.

Sterilization

In the vernacular, the spaying of the bitch is often incorrectly called "sterilization." Because in sterilization, however, only the fallopian tubes are tied, the heat and false pregnancy still occur. For these reasons, sterilization is not customarily performed on the bitch.

Hypersexuality of the male dog

Some male dogs develop a pronounced hypersexual behavior. They mount the owner, strangers, other male dogs, as well as upholstered furniture and anything else they can clasp with their front paws. The best remedy is to neuter the dog.

Neutering the male dog

Neutering cannot take place until after the male dog reaches sexual maturity. Neutering is a simple operation, in which both testicles are removed. The character of the male dog does not change after the operation. Very aggressive behavior patterns, however, will be improved.

Neutered dogs gain weight more readily than do non-neutered dogs. Therefore, feed a third less than before the neutering.

OLD AGE

Thanks to vaccination, veterinary check-ups, and proper nutrition, dogs are living longer and longer today. With good care they live about two to three years longer.

Old age

How quickly a dog becomes old depends on the breed. Large dog breeds are already "senior citizens" from the sixth or seventh year of life on. Small dog breeds have only reached middle age at seven years of age. Accordingly, Great Danes and Saint Bernards usually live only 10 to 12 years, whereas a Dachshund or Poodle can live to 16 to 18 years of age. Mixed breeds live longer on average than do pedigreed dogs.

At what point is the dog old?

Physical and psychological stress can shorten the life of an old dog. For example, older dogs cope poorly with a change of location. Constant noise and commotion in a previously quiet place can put the four-legged friend under constant stress and thereby shorten its life. An old dog no longer tolerates a move as well a younger dog.

What shortens the life of the old dog?

How is old age expressed? The activity of the aging dog decreases. It changes its habits — for example, it sleeps more than before — and forgets acquired behavior patterns. In other words, it becomes "senile." One of the changes is, for example, that previously housebroken dogs suddenly become unhousebroken again. The movements of the old dog become slower, and it becomes more sensitive to heat and cold than before.

A change in body weight also becomes noticeable with age — the old dog either clearly gains weight or becomes distinctly thinner.

What is "old age"? "Old age" is not a disease! It does mean, however, that the powers of regeneration, thus the renewal of all the cells in the body, diminish. As a result, the efficiency of the organs naturally also decreases. Furthermore, in old age the dog is more susceptible to diseases, because the effectiveness of the immune system diminishes.

The hair turns white Approximately from the seventh year of life on, the dog starts to turn gray. The graying begins on the lips and the chin, then extends to the cheeks and nose, and reaches the area around the eyes by about the time the dog is ten years old. As the dog gets even older, the forehead and head also turn gray.

As with humans, with the dog as well there are health disorders that appear with greater frequency in old age.

In old dogs, the thirst reflex is no longer as pronounced as in young dogs. Therefore, they usually drink too little. This leads to the general dehydration of the tissues. This also reduces the kidney function. The urine becomes so concentrated that kidney stones are likely to form. For this reason, always encourage your old four-legged friend to drink. Old dogs that drink little water often readily drink soup, which, however, should not be fatty. You can also mix plenty of lukewarm liquid — for example, water, soup, tea — in the food.

Thirst decreases

When the dog no longer smells and tastes properly, it accordingly eats less. Therefore, some dogs become severely emaciated in old age. Offer the old dog particularly tasty food, and warm it slightly. You can also feed it special "senior diets."

The senses of smell and taste diminish

From about the 12th year of life on, dogs no longer see as acutely as before. This is usually a consequence of the onset of cataracts. With cataracts the lens becomes cloudy and turns milky white. The condition usually begins at the age of eight years, worsens slowly, and is part of the normal aging process.

The eyes weaken

This is actually not so bad for the dog, because as a "scent animal" sharp vision is not as important. Furthermore, it usually takes a very long time for the entire lens to turn completely cloudy. The margins remain transparent for a long time, so that the dog can continue to perceive its sur-

Does the dog suffer from the gradual blindness?

roundings — albeit to a reduced degree — for a long time.

How can you tell if the dog is totally blind?

There is a simple test for this. Lead your dog back and forth a few times in an empty room. Then put an obstacle in its way. If the dog is already totally blind, it will run into it. If it avoids the obstacle, it still has partial vision.

Hearing diminishes

When old dogs become deaf, clogged ear canals are not to blame, but rather the degeneration of the cochlea and the bones of the middle ear. You can provide the dog with slight improvement by giving it regular supplements of vitamins B_{12}, B_1, B_6, and E.

Can the dog survive a stroke?

Following a stroke, the old dog stares straight ahead, circles constantly, wobbles, and is scarcely responsive. Unfortunately, many people still believe that the old dog must now be put to sleep. The fact is that most old dogs survive a stroke very well if they receive timely veterinary treatment.

Why do dogs become "stiff" with age?

After lying down for a fairly long time, many older dogs have a hard time standing up. To blame for this is arthritis, that is, age-related degeneration of the joints. Many old four-legged friends also have problems with their vertebrae. After standing up, they continue to move stiffly for a while. After they warm up, they move visibly more freely.

Cover the dog well while sleeping, because warmth is beneficial with arthritis. The

pad should be thick enough that the cold-
ness of the floor cannot penetrate. Possibly
lay an electric blanket — on a low setting —
on top of it. Do not neglect to consider
veterinary assistance, because certain
medications can at least delay further de-
terioration, if not prevent it completely.

May you walk your "stiff" dog?

Of course, your older dog also needs exercise. You must, however, avoid overload-
ing the damaged joints. Light and regular
physical activity is beneficial. It is better to
walk the old four-legged friend a quarter
hour four times a day than once a day for
an hour. Swimming is ideal, because all
the muscles are involved, but little strain is
put on the joints. And make sure that you
do not overwork your old dog when it has
a good day. It is very bad when your old dog
gets a great deal of exercise one day, and
none at all the next.

Old dog and old heart

If your "senior" four-legged friend coughs
frequently, suffers from shortness of breath,
and creeps around lethargically, it suffers
from an aged heart. After a thorough examination, the veterinarian will prescribe
heart medication. Always administer the
heart medication to the dog at the same
time in the morning. Dogs with an aged
heart can live for many years if they receive
their medication regularly.

Prostate problems

An enlarged prostate leads to difficulties in
defecation and occasionally to blood in the
urine in old male dogs. If your dog suffers
from this, have it neutered as soon as
possible. This is the best therapy.

OLD AGE

Important for the old dog: regular veterinary checkups

From eight years of age on, the dog should have a veterinary checkup twice a year. In this way, age-related organic disease or tumor formation can be recognized and treated in time. The preventive checkup should include a comprehensive blood test, urine test, and a careful examination of the heart.

How much care does the old dog need?

Take plenty of time to care for your old dog. It will reward you for it with a longer life. Brush it particularly thoroughly. This not only produces a beautiful coat, it simultaneously stimulates the circulation. Bathe it now somewhat more frequently than before. Pay particularly close attention to the care of the oral cavity and teeth. Clean your four-legged friend's teeth daily, and have the veterinarian remove tartar. The veterinarian must repair or pull broken teeth, because diseased teeth are sources of infection, promote articular rheumatism, and put a strain on the heart.

When it is time to say good-bye

Even with the most indulgent and best of care, there comes the day when the veterinarian will tell you that your pet's quality of life has fallen to a minimum that can no longer be justified because of its suffering. He will also advise you that further treatment will not extend life, but rather only prolong death. Then you should end the animal's suffering by consenting to having the dog put to sleep (euthanasia). The dog is put to sleep by means of an injection, which is completely painless. Stay with your friend until its last breath, talk to it, and caress it. Then it will gently go to sleep.

DOGGIE GIFTS

There is scarcely a dog owner who does not wish to give his four-legged pet a great pleasure from time to time. This ABC of gifts should give you a few ideas.

Gifts

Leash reels are a gift that the dog will certainly be thankful for. They give the dog more room to move than with a normal leash. You also have the assurance that you can bring the animal back at the touch of a button when necessary.

Leash reels

Address tags for the collar. With them your runaway pet will "find" its way back to you more quickly.

ID tags

Balls: A dog can never have enough. Particularly fun for the dog are balls with built-in bells, but they can be annoying to you. Get a Gumaball®.

Balls

Nylon Bones   Safe nylon bones—Nylabones®—are the best choice for all dogs. These long-lasting chew devices provide hours of entertainment as well as clean teeth and breath.

Rawhide bones   Rawhide bones are very popular with most dogs and have the benefit of delaying the formation of tartar, but they are not always safe as some dogs choke on them. Use Roar-hide® which is rawhide which has been melted and then molded into the shape of a bone.

Puppy bones   Gumabone® is the name for safe, long-lasting polyurethane bones designed for smaller dogs and puppies.

Brushes   Brushes: Brushes suitable for the particular coat are a must for all animals with a beautiful coat.

Complete checkup   Complete checkup at the veterinarian: This is not a "fun" present, but in return all the healthier.

Pet doors   Pet doors: For doors that lead to the back yard. With them your four-legged friend can decide on its own when to go out or come inside. Pet doors are available in the most diverse sizes.

Flea collars   Flea collars provide reliable protection against fleas and thus prevent the unpleasant allergy to fleas.

"Name plate"   Gift certificate for a "name plate" under the skin: A microchip with a unique identification code is inserted under the skin by the veterinarian. This is the most modern, simplest, and safest way to identify animals.

Empty baskets: Puppies feel safe inside them.

Empty baskets

Leather dog boots protect the sensitive paws of your dog in the winter. After all, it is inevitable that chemical thawing agents will be used in the next snow storm.

Leather dog boots

Mice made of genuine mouse skins are great toys for dogs.

Mice

Dishes for food and water are always useful. For large, boisterous dogs, for example, there are extra heavy dishes filled with sand, which do not tip over as easily.

Dishes

Ear-friendly dishes are a special gift for Cocker Spaniels. The dishes are particularly high, and keep the ears from drooping in the food.

Ear-friendly dishes

Water-repellent paw protectants help to prevent cracked foot pads and do good service, particularly in the winter.

Paw protectants

Squeaky toys repeatedly stimulate the play instinct.

Squeaky toys

Rain overalls for Poodles: With these the Poodles not only feels great, it returns home from a walk in the rain dry and clean, after taking the overalls off outside the door.

Rain overalls

DOGGIE GIFTS

Reflective collar Reflective collar: This will increase the safety of your dog in traffic, because it reflects headlights.

Transport bags Transport bags for small dogs are useful time and again, such as on public transportation.

Vitamin drops Vitamin drops are a welcome present for any dog. They contribute to the well-being of the four-legged friend.

Water-proof padded dog coats Waterproof padded dog coats: They are no laughing matter, but rather urgently necessary for older dogs with kidney or ligament disorders.

Tooth-brushes Toothpaste and toothbrushes for dogs prevent dental plaque and thus tartar buildup.

Time Time: Time to play and go for walks is the most wonderful gift of all that you could give to your four-legged pet.

INDEX

INDEX